one step at a time

A tale of purpose, resilience, and determination
From Mount Everest to the Sahara

sébastien sasseville

Tellwell Talent
www.tellwell.ca

ISBN
978-0-2288-0305-8 (Paperback)
978-0-2288-0306-5 (eBook)

To my parents
Christian and Claudette,
my brother Marc-André,
and my sister Geneviève.
Their love and support
have been my greatest
sources of inspiration.

Table of Contents

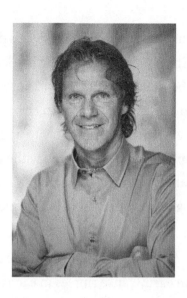

Preface by Pierre Lavoie

Co-founder of the Grand Défi Pierre Lavoie

To Each Their Everest

The first time I met Sébastien Sasseville was in 2010, at the start of the Grand Défi Pierre Lavoie. I had heard about this athlete before, this Ironman who had just scaled the highest peak in the world despite a major handicap: type 1 diabetes. At the time, I thought the same thing as everyone else: "That can't be true!" When I met Sébastien for the first time after one of my talks, I was swept away by this extraordinary man, a true gentleman.

Sébastien refused to be slowed down by his diabetes. He has achieved great things and above all, he has learned valuable lessons, which he shares in this book. These lessons can be applied to the life of anyone who has a cherished dream but does not know where to begin or how to achieve it; anyone who has given up and watches life go on without them; anyone who feels incapable of achieving anything. Of course, anyone who is preparing to scale Everest will also find inspiration in these pages.

In short, One *Step at a Time* is filled with real and inspiring insights that can easily cause ripples in each of our lives.

Sébastien reveals two major facets of his personality in his book: Sébastien the storyteller and Sébastien the motivator. The first goes without saying. When you've reached the summit of Everest, completed six Ironman challenges, and run from one Canadian coast to the other, you can't help but have some fascinating stories to tell, and this book tells many. But he didn't write this book to boast about his exploits. Sébastien did it to show us that the path to the summit teaches us much more than any passing moment of glory ever could. This is where Sébastien stands out as a motivator.

His approach to a challenge is what I found most inspiring about his message. In a world where so many take the easiest path, it's good to hear an alternative. I know from experience that the most difficult part of a challenge like the Ironman is not the competition itself. It's the work that goes into preparing for it and the challenges you must overcome just to reach the starting line, like intense training, time management, professional and family obligations, and injuries, to name a few. What we learn on the road to race day is invaluable. And even if you don't reach the finish line, you will still have experienced something special.

Throughout his incredible journey, Sébastien inspires us to move forward, even if we feel incapable or at a disadvantage. For Sébastien, moving forward has resulted in extraordinary feats. For someone else, walking five kilometres for the first time after years of inactivity is just as remarkable. To each their own Everest.

I love Sébastien's philosophy. He is among those who motivate others to action, and we need people like him. Sébastien is a simple, genuine, and inspiring man, the very image of his book.

Pierre Lavoie
Co-founder of the Grand Défi Pierre Lavoie

Foreword

When we were children, my parents gave me, my sister, and my brother the greatest gift of all: they put us to work at a young age. For the first few years, I complained about this "slavery", but I soon developed a liking for hard work. Our parents' influence shaped our lives, and today I know they are responsible for the ambition that drives all three of us.

This book does not necessarily have a beginning or an end. It's neither a diary, nor an account of my exploits, nor an auto-biography. Instead, each chapter chronicles the lessons I've learned over the years. My ascent of Everest, the race through the Sahara, and my run across Canada are highlights of my life's journey, but they are merely the tip of the iceberg, the visible and most spectacular portion of a long inner journey. The lessons I've picked up along the way have always been simple and accessible to anyone, as long as they're paying close attention. Feel free to browse the table of contents and read only the chapters that seem most interesting to you.

Over the years, I've learned to be more attuned to signs in my environment, to pay attention to messages from the universe, and to find the lessons hidden within those messages. I learned consistency from watching the shifting dunes, and discipline from crossing glaciers. I learned how to learn. Whether we wear Oxfords or cleats, we all face extremely similar challenges. Every day, we face an environment, a climate, competition, and conditions that are in constant change. The obvious parallels between sports, business, and our personal lives are filled with meaning and are always undeniably useful. Through this book, I hope to share my passion for learning.

In order to learn, we must first cultivate openness, humility, a state of mind that encourages growth, and a willingness to learn based on acknowledged imperfection. Many of us want to learn, to grow, to improve. Just like a gardener prepares the soil before planting seeds, it is important that we prepare ourselves to learn and make sure we are in a positive state of mind. Otherwise, our efforts will be in vain. Lessons learned don't stick, changes in behaviour are fleeting, and old habits die hard. At first, these truths were only gibberish.

My first years in the real world were chaotic. For a long time, I blocked and sabotaged personal growth in any form. Eventually, with a few scratches, lots of work, and several setbacks, I slowly absorbed many ideas about success and growth. Through this book, I want to help you avoid all the detours I took and the mistakes I made. My intention is not to tell you what I've done, but rather to share what I've learned.

Adopting habits for personal growth, harmony between yourself and your goals, and the concept each person has of success, failure, and how they are measured are at the heart of this book. In business and at home, we face countless points of resistance every day. I give talks around the world, motivated by the desire to help companies and organizations develop a culture of excellence. Here, as on stage, I will begin by recounting a story from my adventures, and from there share the significance of that story and how its lesson can be applied to either the business world or our personal lives, but most often to both.

We are often tempted to ask those who have enjoyed great success or accomplished something amazing about their magic formula. Social media is full of articles about the "five habits of successful entrepreneurs" or "six things rich people do every day". But I believe that it's not enough to draw a direct line between certain actions and success. My experience of success has been much more like a whirlwind of events than a straight line, more a dance than a recipe. Success is a dance with obstacles, resistance (both chosen and imposed), a destination (physical or figurative), a desire to grow, many measures of success, a quest, a path to follow, and many other factors.

At the end of the day, these efforts are all for happiness, aren't they? Happiness is not something that we seek, it's a decision we must make every morning. If I were to venture to define it, I would call it a state of satisfaction in the quest for perpetually unfinished growth. The main elements are clear: a quest, growth, non-completion. Happiness therefore involves accepting imperfection and enjoying the journey more than the destination.

I've experienced a lot, even though I haven't even reached my forties. I know what the world looks like from the peak of Mount Everest. My legs have known pain that few will experience, caused by running 170 marathons in nine months. Scaling mountains, I twice felt certain that my death was imminent, only to then experience euphoria, an indescribable joy more powerful than any drug, the simple joy of being alive. I witnessed the pride of accomplishment in the eyes of dozens of teens that I guided in Nepal and on the slopes of Kilimanjaro. I've travelled across the planet, and I've crossed the finish line of many triathlons. I once spent five days running across the Sahara, in a vast emptiness where the mercury hit 42 degrees Celsius and where I had to carry everything on my back. None of this matters. None of this represents success.

These moments are points in time, brief blips that never last long. I am proud of them, but if you buy me a drink, they won't be the stories I'll tell you. The quest, the transformation, the desire to grow, the joy in trying, the choosing of a destination to move forward, and the lessons learned from my worst days, these are what fascinate me.

An anonymous author once said happiness is in the effort we make. We are often told that the journey is more important than the destination, and I wholeheartedly agree. But I would add that even more important than the journey is the meaning we give to it. I've taken many steps on my journey. I've fallen, failed, taken countless steps in the wrong direction. Other steps were glorious, lauded, historic. What I've done is not important.

Here is what I've learned.

Sébastien

Outset

I've travelled all over the world, keeping my distance from tourist hotspots as much as possible. I wanted to see the people, their customs, and their reality. Around the globe, regardless of language, continent, country, or religion, I've noticed that school children always form teams the same way. Two captains are appointed, usually the most popular students in the class. They take turns picking who will be on their team. They choose and choose and choose, until there is only one person left, humiliated before the game has even begun.

For the first 15 years of my life, I was the kid that everyone picked last. Like any good book or speech, it is appropriate that I begin by disclosing my conflict of interest: I am not very athletically gifted. In fact, I am awful at sports. I've never stood on a podium, I've never even won a race or a medal. This is all to say that I am not very athletically gifted, and yet have been successful in this domain. It's a subtle but crucial difference, because it reminds us that hard work and perseverance prevail over natural talent.

I think it's important to announce this right at the start. There are some who think I'm a born athlete, that I was the captain of all the sports teams when I was a kid. They couldn't be further from the truth. I was tall and thin, I had no coordination, no endurance, and no physical strength. In short, I was not athlete material at all. I do not come from a rich family. I grew up in a small town of barely one thousand inhabitants, in a middle-class family, so most of my globetrotting adventures were paid for by others. Each adventure was paid for by a sponsorship, which took a lot of hard work to obtain.

For many years, I ran only because I was late or because I was being chased by someone bigger than I was. It wasn't until I was in my twenties that I began to introduce fitness and racing into my life.

When I was just starting to run, I quickly noticed that my pace would quicken whenever my favourite song came on. Not only did I pick up speed, but I was overcome with a feeling of euphoria and a temporary impression of increased strength, as though the music was giving me wings and awakening feelings of pure bliss, power, and invincibility within me. I suddenly had access to unexpected energy, as if, for a moment, I were much more in shape than I really was. For the length of one song, I could run far beyond my abilities, and even appreciated the extra effort, as if it were being transformed into joy.

Not a runner? This experience is not unique to running. Think about when you're busy doing chores and your favourite song starts to play. Suddenly, the task seems less monotonous, and in a few seconds, you forget everything and almost enjoy vacuuming.

A few years later, during my first competitions, I felt the same emotion as I approached the finish line. Once the end was in sight, I was sprinting! Taken by that same feeling of invincibility, I crossed the finish line at full speed. All runners sprint when they see the finish line. It's a universal experience and traverses all borders. It's funny, but sometimes we try to convince the crowd that we've run the whole race at that speed, despite the stopwatch telling a completely different story.

So I started to wonder about this phenomenon. First, how could we replicate this feeling of strength and access it on demand, as often as we wanted? And, if this feeling could be accessed at any time, what goals could we set for ourselves and our businesses? No doubt we would set the bar a little higher. Would we face adversity and obstacles with a different attitude?

A life where our favourite song plays continuously. That's what we should aspire to create every day. It has been by choosing to face the obstacle head on instead of trying to avoid it that I've learned the most. Today, thanks to the many lessons I've learned, I feel this strength most of the time.

My journey has been simple and very human. In fact, there's nothing simpler: just an ordinary guy who gets up early, works hard, and does extraordinary things. That's all. I want to tell my story because I want to share my belief that anyone can achieve the best version of themselves. I have always believed that I could do whatever I put my mind to and succeed if I only worked hard enough and long enough. We are all destined for success, for great achievements, for a legacy that lives beyond us. Note that I did not "develop a belief" that we can all accomplish anything we want to. I "discovered" that we can all accomplish almost anything we want to. These are two very different feelings.

This discovery has an incredible transformative power. Many books will devote hundreds of pages to convince us of our potential, our unlimited potential. This book *begins* by accepting the premise that we can all accomplish great things and that we all have unlimited potential. The question, then, is to know what you will make of this potential. What will you create and build? What will be your first step tomorrow, and what goal will you be walking towards? What legacy will you leave behind, and what will we remember about you once you have passed from our lives?

All this being said, the saying "anything is possible" is wrong. Not everything is possible. A person with a severe disability cannot win gold in the 100-metre sprint. Some people grow up in tragic family situations that limit their access to opportunities. Others are born into extreme poverty or in developing countries, and their mere survival is a miracle. Let's make one thing clear: we are not all born with the same luck, the same resources, or the same abilities. The circumstances of your birth are often a significant determiner of your access to opportunities, and life is something of a lottery. Simply being able to tell yourself that with a lot of effort anything is possible is a luxury. We must accept this privilege with great gratitude and avoid wasting this chance.

What makes something great?

If it's your thing, it's a great thing. By expanding and diversifying our scale, we learn that the only important quest is to push ourselves further. How can I develop to my full potential? What am I capable of? Don't measure yourself by how fast you can run, but by the progress you have made since the first step. Don't compare your modest savings to your neighbour's millions; be proud of having broken the cycle of poverty in your family. Your degree of happiness or success is always directly linked to how you measure it. Don't let anyone else decide how you measure your success. Who chose the scale you use to measure your life today? You or someone else?

One of the pitfalls of today's society is that we let others, often false gurus, celebrities, or even our peers, define what success should mean to us.

> Don't let anyone else decide how
> you measure your success.

So, even if we aren't all born with the same opportunities, we all have the power to achieve great things. There are no small challenges, less valid causes, or insignificant achievements. At conferences, people often approach me by saying, "I'm preparing for a half marathon, which is probably nothing for you, but..." Wrong! First, a half marathon is not nothing for me. Like I said, I've never stood on a podium. Also, what it means for me really doesn't matter. If it's your thing, it's a great thing. What matters is not how high you climb or how fast you run. What makes an action or a process great is the transformation you experience along the way.

The Power of the Dream

I was 21 years old. I was a student, and my biggest dream was to travel all over the world. One morning in January 2001, I heard the irresistible call of Asia, a feeling that was as powerful as it was impossible to explain. More than that, I didn't feel I had to justify it. This deep conviction that I had to travel to Asia was even comforting, as though I had been promised I would find answers there.

The human mind is constantly in search of understanding. We want to understand everything, explain everything. Science and medicine explain many strange phenomena, diseases, and laws of physics. We seek to expand our knowledge every day. Psychology tries to explain the mind, the intangible, and our behaviour. Humans even invented a box called "God" to put everything they don't understand into and thus explain it.

I love this quote from author and poet Rainer Maria Rilke:

"I beg you, to have patience with everything unresolved in your heart and to try to love the questions themselves as if they were locked rooms or books written in a very foreign language. Don't search for the answers, which could not be given to you now, because you would not be able to live them. And the point is to live everything. Live the questions now. Perhaps then, someday far in the future, you will gradually, without even noticing it, live your way into the answer."

That winter morning, I was blessed with a great gift: the call of the dream. We all hear these calls, which we call signs. Answering these calls and following our own path always begins with a leap of faith and confidence in the path we're on. By accepting that we do not instantly have all the answers, we allow our destiny to manifest more freely. It's not an invitation to complacency or a suggestion that our destiny will be fulfilled by the flick of a magic wand, or even a proposition that someone should wait for a moment of illumination to act. However, sooner or later, we all have moments of clarity when the call seems obvious. Many of us turn our backs to the call, succumbing to fear, often because we don't immediately understand it. Following our path also means accepting that we won't have all the answers at the beginning.

The dream is powerful. The dream, but especially the fire it kindles, is often even more alluring than the accomplishment. This story is funny to me, but it's also a great example of what

I mean. After I ascended Everest, my friends developed a very bad habit of introducing me to women by mentioning that feat. I hated it, and I still do. People rarely react positively to any mention of Everest. Women believed my friends were exaggerating or outright lying.

The irony is that I had much more success before Everest! I was proud of my dream. The fire, the determination, and the desire to succeed that drove me were palpable and, apparently, very attractive.

The lesson here is that the dream is often much more enticing than the accomplishment. This is true for those who live alongside us, but also for ourselves. The idea that once Everest was behind me I returned home with a newly acquired unshakable confidence is completely wrong. It was during the journey that I realized my full potential, that I was transformed, not at the summit.

The journey, the road, or the experience is often more attractive than the accomplishment.

Whatever your dream is, it is powerful. Climbing Everest or starting a business, travelling the world or writing a book, participating in the Olympics or becoming a dentist: when it's true, when it's yours, the dream is always great. The dream brings people together, and it's contagious. Indeed, we love inspiring people precisely because of their infectious powers.

By following their journeys and following their dreams, we are inspired to follow our own and believe in our own potential.

Let's get back to the winter of 2001. Answering the call, I bought a plane ticket to Asia a few days later. I was scheduled to leave in May, a few days after the winter semester would end. Destination: Bangkok. Since I was studying at university during the day, I took an evening job to pay for my trip. Logical, right?

Months later, a book caught my eye in Chiang Mai, in northern Thailand: *Trekking in the Nepal Himalaya*. As before, the call was strong. Fascinated by Everest since childhood, I saw this as another sign. Unable to resist the call, and without any desire to resist, I travelled to Nepal with the intention of walking right into Everest Base Camp.

In Kathmandu, the capital, I discovered an incredible city. Colours, smells, and noises came together to create a cacophony that shifted between organization and complete chaos. I took a lot of pictures, on film at the time. For most trekkers, the journey towards Base Camp begins at Lukla and takes approximately 10 days. Since I couldn't afford the legendary flight across the Himalayas to Lukla, I took a bus to Jiri for a few dollars. The bus was crowded of course, occupied by Nepalis, merchandise, poultry, and small livestock. It was an unforgettable 11 hours, filled with colour, along narrow and winding mountain roads. From Jiri, I had to walk for about 10 days across the mountainous terrain to reach Lukla, which gave me plenty of opportunities to see the best of what the country had to offer.

In the days that followed, I took the first steps towards Everest Base Camp. Because it was the off-season, I was completely alone, going head-to-head with the Goliath that would completely change my life. Everything became clear: I felt a call to come to Asia to build a connection with the mountain. There I found a mission, a destination, a desire to grow, explore, and discover, both on the mountain and within myself. After many hours of contemplating the highest peak in the world, I returned home, promising to myself that one day, I'd come back to climb to the summit.

At 22, one year after my first trip to Asia, my world was turned upside down. I was experiencing unusual fatigue throughout the academic term. I was taking naps after meals, I had no energy, and I was losing a lot of weight. My symptoms were getting worse, but I attributed the fatigue to my studies and to the busy life that I led. In May 2002, much more alarming symptoms appeared: blurred vision, loss of appetite, significant weight loss, extreme thirst, and frequent urination. In the days preceding my diagnosis, I could drink a litre of water and feel thirsty again within minutes. I was urinating three, four, or five times every hour. Accepting the signs, I spoke to a doctor in May 2002 and was diagnosed with type 1 diabetes.

Type 1 diabetes is a condition that cannot be prevented or cured. It is not brought on by nutrition or a lack of physical activity; it's an autoimmune disease, a disruption of the immune system. Think of it this way: the soldiers that normally protect us from viruses and other attacks lose their map and end up attacking the body. In my case, they were angry with my pancreas, the gland that produces insulin.

In general, people are much more familiar with type 2 diabetes, which people usually know about through their grandmothers or portly uncles. In fact, 90% of people with diabetes have type 2 diabetes, which can be prevented or at least delayed with healthy lifestyles, healthful food choices, and regular physical exercise.

Only 10% of people with diabetes have type 1 diabetes, formerly called juvenile diabetes because in the past it always occurred at a young age. Without knowing precisely why, medical science has found that it appears at almost any age. In short, I developed type 1 diabetes overnight.

Upon diagnosis, everything changes and everything stops at the same time. Being hospitalized is never pleasant, but at least when you return home, it's usually because you've been cured. But when you have a chronic illness like type 1 diabetes, you go home with a new life.

I didn't know it yet, but my life had just been blessed with something wonderful. I had received an amazing gift, an indispensable tool, and an incredibly powerful motor.

Insulin-dependent for the rest of my days, I now wear a permanent insulin pump to live. I have to check my blood sugar several times a day and constantly make calculations to balance my blood sugar, ingested carbohydrates, physical exercise, and other variables, which is what makes the condition so difficult to manage. It's hard work and lots of effort, and it complicates everything I do.

Despite that, I've never managed to be dramatic about it. My story would probably be more interesting or profitable if it had a great moment of darkness, refusal, or denial following my diagnosis. After the initial shock, I realized within a few days that this obstacle was forcing me to grow, to think differently, and to adapt. Ironically, I saw my diagnosis as a reason to monitor my health. Life forced me to stop going out to pubs, exercise more, and eat healthy foods. I decided to jump on this opportunity without looking back. There was no debate, no nostalgia, no looking back to the past. It was simple.

A common claim is that it takes a certain type of personality, wisdom, determination, or resilience to make this choice. Honestly, I disagree. The undeniable fact is that I had just been diagnosed with type 1 diabetes. I had no control over it, and I had no choice in the matter. I was standing on a train track, and a train was bearing down on me. All I did was choose to hop on rather than stay on the track and wait for the train to hit me. There was nothing ingenious about this choice.

15 years after my diagnosis, after a long period of reflection, I like to say that the condition has been an incredible gift. However, when I think about it, it was not the illness that was the gift, but the fact that I was not given a choice.

Today, even if I could reverse the condition, I wouldn't change a thing. It has become a valuable ally. There are many things I hate about my condition, small annoyances that I would like to see disappear, but I would hate to lose the drive that the condition has given me, the push for self-discovery and exploration, the push for growth. Like physical training, this drive can be a source of pain. However, it is also a source of learning and contributes to my physical, psychological, and intellectual development.

It would be a tragedy if I became unable to be physically active, because I've learned so much through sport. The loss of opportunities would be just as significant if my condition were removed from me. Unfortunately, we can't always choose what drives us, but we can decide what we will do with it and where it will take us.

Energy results from a force opposing a resistance. We do not always choose the obstacles, but we can choose the strength that we exert on them. The bigger the obstacle, the bigger the potential.

The sad truth is that thousands of people and families have had a completely different experience with diabetes. I've seen lives broken simply because people never accepted their condition. Learning to see it as an ally is a long process. I've put in time and I still work at it every day. However, accepting it is easier than you think, and it starts, first and foremost, with accepting certain undeniable facts, rather than fighting against them.

In my diagnosis I saw a gift and an opportunity for growth. I quickly realized that my perspective was unique. I wanted to convey it, to share it. Suddenly, my desire to climb Everest had meaning; my condition had given it meaning. The goal, initially very personal and very focused on the glory of the achievement, became much larger and much more noble. The physical feat had not become more important, but its meaning had. Over the years, it would be precisely from that meaning that I would draw the energy to continue.

The First Step

It takes almost two months to reach the summit of Everest. I ascended in 2008. From Kathmandu, a 60-minute flight takes you to Lukla, a small mountainside village at 2,850 metres above sea level. Barely after leaving the Nepalese capital, the flight becomes a treacherous slalom between the Himalayan mountain peaks. Thrill seekers will also enjoy the landing. The runway is a rising slope, right along the mountainside, and ends in a sharp drop to nothing: a cliff, dozens of metres high. Landings and takeoffs are given no room for error. Most would grant this non-pressurized flight the honour of the most perilous and spectacular flight in the world.

The remote area offers a beautifully soothing atmosphere. There are no roads or vehicles, just hundreds of kilometres of trails that connect dozens of small communities lost among the mountains and in their valleys. You feel a sense of awe from the first moment you set foot here.

A 10-day hike separates Lukla from Everest Base Camp. The trek is one of the most popular in the world, and hundreds of trekkers undertake this journey every year. The trail is spectacular. The Himalayas towering above you are a breathtaking sight, and a powerful energy emanates from the mountains. The hike itself is incredibly demanding. Each day brings its own series of ascents and descents, and very early on, the altitude makes the task very challenging. However, the effort is worthwhile, and the beauty of the region quickly makes trekkers forget the pain of the journey.

A few days after leaving Lukla, you'll reach Namche Bazaar, a stunning and picturesque village. At 3,400 metres above sea level, extending in a crescent along the slope of the mountain, perched hundreds of metres above a valley and capped by snowy peaks, this village seems to be straight out of a fantasy film. Dozens of merchants spend their days on the hike between Lukla and Namche Bazaar, carrying many pounds of merchandise on their shoulders. Through them, Namche Bazaar and the small surrounding villages are always well supplied. Even technology has found its way to Namche Bazaar, which now enjoys internet access.

From here to Base Camp, breaks are essential to acclimatize your body to the lower oxygen levels in the air. Namche Bazaar, with its local craft shops, its divine chocolate cake, and, it bears repeating, its internet access, is the perfect spot to spend a couple days for the first break. Another acclimatization break will be required a few days later at Pheriche, a tiny village of just 15 people at 4,200 metres above sea level.

Not without some sweat, we arrived at Base Camp in early April 2008. It takes 10 days of hard hiking just to get to where everything begins. The right to be on the starting line must be earned. In high altitudes, there is nothing gained by going fast. In fact, the more slowly you ascend, the better your body acclimatizes. Very early on in the expedition, before even reaching Base Camp, everything you do has an impact on your performance on the mountain.

People ask me the same question after every talk I give: *What's next?* I definitely have ideas, but before ever setting foot on the starting line of a major project, there's a long planning phase to get through. The project has to be built from scratch. This is the invisible part of a project, and it's also the most difficult. It's when you're told *no* 30 times before hearing a positive response to a request for funding. It's when you have to work on your projects every weekend and evening, since you have to work a day job to survive. It's when you work to the detriment of your social life and your free time to spend with family.

At the start of my twenties, I made every possible mistake as I looked for sponsors. Today, I have a lot of expertise in this area, and I've managed to secure funding for projects to the tune of millions of dollars in the past few years. It's an art that could be the subject of a whole separate book. I've learned a lot from the mistakes I've made and the time I've invested. Throughout this planning stage, I was making my way not to the finish line, but to the starting line. The fire that motivates us when we complete a project is especially important during planning, because that's the true test.

As of now, I've completed six Ironman triathlons, which differ from the classic triathlon in that they take place over a total distance of 226 kilometres. I've come close to my dream of breaking ten hours, missing the target by mere minutes. These competitions are a symbol of endurance, and the athletes who pass the test can hold their heads high for the rest of their lives. We focus on how these super athletes perform on the day of the challenge, but the real test of a triathlon is not to overcome the challenge: it is first and foremost to reach the starting line. Race day is a celebration of the athlete's training, a demonstration of what it has made possible. The real challenge, the aspect that requires superhuman discipline and endless determination, is the training itself. The months and years of training required to survive a triathlon is the real accomplishment.

Champions aren't made on the day of the competition. They're made in training.

> The starting line is not a right, it's a privilege that must be earned.

Everest commands respect. However, climbers mostly agree that it's not a very technical climb. The challenge is in the altitude, the long period spent on the mountain, exposed to the elements, and above all, the complexity of organizing the expedition and the sacrifices it requires. It takes years of training, sacrifice, and planning. It's not talent that separates people who achieve great things from the rest. Rather, it's their focus and their ability to commit to a long-term goal. Talent is born from our genetic makeup. Our focus and the persistence of our commitment are consciously chosen, developed, and maintained by us.

Focus always takes precedent over talent.

A stubborn fool will go much further in life than a genius with no perseverance. At birth, the physical capacities of Olympic athletes are not very different from those of the rest of us. However, they have an unwavering ability to stay focused on a target for years. They know how to direct all the support and resources available to them towards practicing an action or routine until it's perfect. For a summit or a finish line to exist some day, the starting line must be carefully planned. Before winning the privilege of trying to succeed, your spot on the starting line must be earned.

The first step is always the most powerful. On February 2, 2014, I found myself on a starting line. Before me, 7,200 kilometres, nine months of running to the tune of five or six marathons per week, in every kind of weather you can imagine. The scene was exciting. Cameras from all the major networks were there. Family and friends were gathered, a small crowd had amassed at the top of Signal Hill in St.

John's, Newfoundland and Labrador, to witness my departure. A magical touch was added by the 20 or so young people, all with type 1 diabetes, who would join me for the first kilometre of this historic marathon. It was beautiful! I was proud and excited, but inside, I was terrified. A voice inside me kept saying, *What a horrible idea!*

On the surface, my achievements all seem very different from one another: from Everest to the Sahara, from frozen landscapes to extreme heat. How does a person become an expert in their discipline, and how do they return to zero the next day to earn success in a whole different world? But when I look closer, I can see that all my achievements have two things in common. Each one always began with a dream, a goal, or a destination that felt completely impossible and that terrified me, and each always started with a single step, so small that it seemed completely insignificant and useless.

At the risk of repeating myself, what I've done is not important. The story I tell to companies is what happens between the first step and the last. To my great surprise, the most powerful step on Everest was not the last. All my life, I had dreamed of the day when I would set foot on the roof of the world and take a deep breath, bursting with pride as I looked to the horizon. I thought that the last step would be the punctuation mark that would complete the adventure and give it meaning. I had dreamed of the day when I would be able to say that I was part of an exclusive club of mountain climbers who had climbed to the top of the world.

Of course, that last step was filled with emotion. But the most powerful step, the one that was most memorable, was without a doubt the first step I took out of Base Camp, the first of thousands upon thousands of steps that would take me to the top of the world. This was my third visit to Nepal. My previous mountain climbing trips all over the world had been preparing me for this great expedition. For almost ten years, I invested every ounce of energy and passion that I had into this ascension. Two months of work still separated me from the peak, and there was certainly no guarantee that I would succeed. My biggest dream was to ascend Everest, and with this single step above Base Camp, the dream was in the bag. I was in the process of climbing this mountain.

If your dream is to write a book, start with one word. If you are overweight and dream of running a marathon, start by walking. Commitment comes before success. Success in business always starts with a first step.

The first step is powerful, because by taking that step our convictions are transformed. With the first step, we pledge to make possible tomorrow that which is impossible today. It has a significant impact on our perceptions, our beliefs, and our future actions.

The first step is a leap of faith, a promise to trust in the future and in ourselves that gives rise to a commitment that transcends words. It sends a signal to the universe that we are ready to learn, to fail, to fall, to get back up, and to grow. It is powerful because not only is it a commitment, it also makes it irreversible. The most difficult part of a marathon is never the marathon itself; it's signing up. Once you're registered, you've committed yourself, and it's amazing how much easier everything becomes! You run a few times per week, you ask questions, you learn, you have good days and bad days, and, one morning, you show up at the marathon and you run! It's as simple as that.

In St. John's, Newfoundland and Labrador, on February 2, 2014, I was on the starting line with thousands of kilometres ahead of me. The task was monumental, absurd even: a journey of 7,200 kilometres that would take more than nine months to complete. Our resumes don't matter on the starting line. I had reached the summit of Mount Everest a few years earlier, but on this starting line, I was afraid: afraid of failure, afraid of not being up to the task. I felt vulnerable and I didn't know how I would succeed.

On that cold February morning, I took the first step with a young man named Thomas in mind. In a sense, it was thanks to him that I was on the starting line. The year before, I received a very touching email from his mother, who wrote that her five-year-old diabetic son was experiencing difficulty in his life. He had gotten sick with the flu, and depression was quietly overpowering him. At times, he asked his mother what he had done to God to deserve his condition, feeling a sort of regret for something he might have done. His mother, saddened but determined to help, gave him several examples of people with diabetes who were making great achievements in their lives, including me. She showed him my website and photos of my Mount Everest ascent, and a light returned to his eyes. He told her, "Mom, I want to meet him."

I was very touched and I felt like I had no right to refuse to meet him. If a simple meeting could have a positive impact on his life, then I had the duty to go visit him. The meeting was wonderful in every way. I met the family several times, and Thomas became more physically active and started to manage his diabetes. It's thanks in part to that meeting that I realized that there must have been thousands of children like Thomas across the country. I realized that by running across the country for this cause, I would have the opportunity to meet and spend a few minutes with them.

On the starting line, I was afraid and I didn't know whether I would succeed in running all the way to Vancouver. It is thanks to Thomas that I realized that it's better to use your energy to find meaning in what you do than to avoid discomfort. Thomas helped me understand that the cost of not trying is much greater than the price of failure.

On a cold and damp Sunday in February in St. John's, Newfoundland and Labrador, with Thomas and all those who shared his situation in mind, without even knowing whether I would succeed, I started my run across Canada.

You don't have to have all the answers before taking the first step and making a change.

You don't have to have all the answers before initiating change. Taking the first step is accepting that you don't have all the answers now and deciding to find them on the way. Taking the first step is trusting in your path and believing that you will find the answers there. When I think back to my state of mind at the start of that crossing, the first thing I think of is that I had no idea what I had signed up for! It's an expression we hear a lot. However, the adventure was extraordinary, filled with lessons and discoveries, precisely because I had no idea what I was getting into! That's the kind of adventure we should seek out every day of our lives, in both our professional and personal lives.

Oftentimes, the reason we don't take the first step is that the last step—and especially what it represents—scares us.

As I've already said, for a long time I ran only when I was late or when I was being followed. Did the idea of completing a triathlon, of scaling Everest, of racing across the Sahara, or worse, of running 7,200 kilometres terrify me? Of course it did! But all that is the last step.

Did the idea of signing up for a climbing class for beginners, every Tuesday evening from 7 to 8 p.m. intimidate me? Not at all. That was the first step.

Never let the last step prevent you from taking the first step.

When I'm ready... Next year... I'm waiting until I have more experience... I'll sign up for this race once I've done more training...

That familiar voice is what stops us from taking the first step, from signing up, or from committing ourselves. The voice that says "when I'm ready" is that part of us that wants to wait to be sure that we won't fail. That moment will never arrive. Such certainty doesn't exist, and if it did, life would be dull.

Meanwhile, we waste time and delay our progress.

When I give talks at companies, I'm often asked to speak about failure and my opinion of it. Nobody can resist the temptation; everyone wants simple and practical tips for overcoming failure, as though I had a magic wand. However, it's not about accepting, taming, or overcoming failure. It's about changing how you think of failure.

When we look for tricks to overcome failure, we are treating the symptom instead of the disease. Instead of learning to overcome failure, we must change our perception of it. We only fear things that are negative, so if we view failure as positive, we will stop fearing it.

Failure is an opportunity for learning, a joyous occasion, a key point that highlights what we need to adapt to succeed and win.

When a scientist has a brilliant idea, they are delighted. That brilliant idea often comes to them after an experiment that did not go as planned. If experiments always turned out as planned, they would no longer be experiments, but simple exercises of measurement and validation. It is failure alone that, by shedding light on what does not work, can cause an ingenious idea to germinate.

Taking the first step means welcoming future failures and waiting gratefully for them, knowing that it's only through failure that we move forward.

Failure is the fuel of success.

The finish line is sometimes like a magnet. It obsesses us and draws us towards it, encourages us to continue, helps us persevere. The starting line is the springboard that propels us forward.

Warm-Up

Beyond the message of hope, the campaign for diabetes, and the people both young and old that I wanted to inspire, my run across Canada was also the journey of a lifetime with my friend Patrick St-Martin. For nine months drove alongside me in a truck, one kilometre at a time. Sharing a picnic in a stunning landscape every day, laughing constantly, we were like children who just wanted to have fun. We lived a year on the road together, almost every night and day. It was an unforgettable experience. We could always count on each other when times were tough, and our relationship was forever changed by this adventure.

It can take years of effort to earn the right to a spot on the starting line. Whether it's one marathon or 170, a change of career or buying a cottage, each starting line has a price, which is paid with sacrifices, sweat, doubts, perseverance, and conviction. On January 27, Patrick left Quebec behind the wheel of the official campaign truck, towing our 10-metre trailer. A few days earlier, we had narrowly avoided a collision that would have destroyed the trailer, which had just been freshly painted with the campaign colours. The last-minute preparations were a mad dash, and the stress and pressure were enormous.

At the end of January, I flew to St. John's, Newfoundland. I arrived three days before my journey was to begin, and was immediately harried by media coverage, interviews, the documentary shooting, and so on. It was an overwhelming and exhausting sprint, far from ideal for the physical preparation required for such a challenge.

The day before departure, everything was ready to go. Without having taken even a single step, we had accomplished the impossible: convinced four multinational companies to invest $500,000 for a man with type 1 diabetes to cross Canada over nine months, to plan a total of 41 events across the country. We had planned and launched a public relations campaign to shoot a documentary, and to articulate a strong and concise message that would resonate with people throughout the country over those nine months. It was about 7 p.m. on February 1, 2014, the day before the big departure. The documentary team, Patrick, and I toasted our achievement in a pub on famous George Street in St. John's, Newfoundland and Labrador. I was proud, as were we all. Besides celebrating our accomplishment, all the pressure we had been under for the past year was easing as well.

My starting line was at the top of Signal Hill, a small hill that overlooks the Atlantic Ocean and the city of St. John's. Some 60 people had answered the call. The crowd was joyous and excited, and young people with diabetes were enthusiastic about being able to run the first kilometre with me. A strong image, a journey announced with a great deal of fanfare: everything was perfect.

St. John's is a small city, so I quickly reached the Trans-Canada Highway. Barely begun, the campaign was already deeply moving. I will never forget the first time I found myself alone on the highway, after everyone else had fallen back. Each day of the campaign left unforgettable memories, but this one has remained one of the most striking. The microphones and cameras had suddenly disappeared. The weather was grim, and I was all alone in the cold and wet climate of Newfoundland, escorted by a vehicle with flashing orange lights.

It was then that I realized the true nature of the challenge; there was the physical part, of course, but there was also the isolation, which would be the most difficult aspect for me. The task ahead of me suddenly seemed insurmountable. Each step was already tough, and I would have to run more than 200 kilometres every week for the next nine months. The outside world and the media would draw a dramatic portrait of the challenge. But the truth was that I would be left alone with my own mind for many months, slowly pressing forward through the wilderness and in all weather conditions. Whatever people would say, my days were not very illustrious. Without realizing it, I was entering into a meditative state that would last almost a full year.

The first part of the journey was what I now call the adolescent phase of the campaign. There are no instructions for this kind of adventure, and we had to improvise and figure out how to do it as we went along. Overflowing with energy, neither Patrick nor I fully understood our luck.

For me to run across Canada, and for the message I wanted to share to be heard loud and clear, we needed the support of a great team. My cross-Canada run was the result of the collaboration of hundreds of people, near and far. My local library did not have a yellow book called *How to Run Across Canada for Dummies*. The sponsors, partners, volunteers, Patrick, and I all found ourselves in uncharted territory.

The more we innovate and the more we try to overcome our limits or change things, the more we find ourselves in an unknown land. When we try much more, we necessarily fail much more.

> A decision to innovate is a decision to
> fail until you find what works.

It's simple, logical, inevitable, and beneficial. It's true in business, it's true in our personal lives, and it was true from the start of the campaign. And since failure is inevitable, we must prepare for it to benefit from it, and therefore, we must learn to fail with grace.

I meet with business executives as part of my job as a public speaker. The mistake I see most often is ordering innovation without first creating a climate to foster it.

Suppose that you want to cultivate cucumbers. Even with the best seeds in the world, even if they were genetically modified, even if they produced cucumbers three feet long, if you drop the seeds onto cement, they will not germinate. They will not grow. Conversely, without even sowing any seeds, plants will rapidly take root wherever the soil is fertile. What I tell business executives is that innovation is not ordered, it is harvested. Work hard on creating a judgment-free climate that encourages new ideas, a psychologically safe climate that does not punish failure. The result is creativity and innovation.

Punishing failure is how a company kills innovation.

As manager of the cross-Canada run, my goal was to create a safe climate where every team member could fail successfully. To survive the first part of the crossing and above all to strengthen the team, I had to let the team benefit from failure.

In order for a team to succeed, it must
be able to operate in a climate where all
its members may fail with success.

I wanted every member of the team, both volunteers and sponsors, to understand that failure is actually a point of resistance packed with lessons anyone can use. I wanted to instill a safe climate focused on growth, where failures would never be covered up. I did not want failures to belong to individuals, but to the whole team to propel it forward.

Patrick drove the official truck from Quebec to Newfoundland and Labrador, dropping off the trailer in Nova Scotia along the way, since we wouldn't be able to use it during the winter. For the first two months of the campaign, we stayed in hotel rooms, most of them offered free of charge. Newfoundlander hospitality knows no limits. By far the most generous province in the country, people stopped the truck every day to donate to support us.

I ran across Canada from coast to coast. I did not go from town to town for a PR stunt and a few loops for a few extra kilometres, only to drive to the next location. I literally ran from Newfoundland to British Columbia.

Logistically speaking, our routine was fairly simple. I ran approximately 40 kilometres per day for three consecutive days, followed by a rest day. This translates to five or six marathons every week for nine months. Patrick escorted me when possible, or otherwise waited for me five kilometres ahead. Since the Trans-Canada Highway does not necessarily have hotels every 40 kilometres, we would return to the same spot, known as base camp, for about a week. For the first few months, it was hotels, and after that, we enjoyed luxury camping in the trailer. At the end of each day of running, I would stop at an intersection, an address, or a specific landmark before heading back to base camp in the campaign vehicle. The next day, Patrick would drop me off at the spot where I had stopped the day before, and I would start running from there.

The idea was to set up base camp in the middle of the leg I planned to run for a week in order to optimize our movements. Each week, we set up a new camp at the most strategic location, then retraced our steps in the truck, driving sometimes over 100 kilometres to return to the starting line for that day's marathon. I would then run for 40 kilometres, and we would have only 60 kilometres to drive back to base camp in the evening.

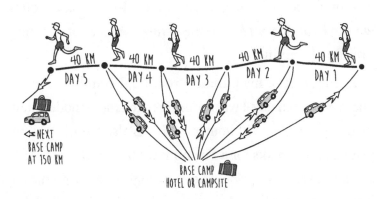

Once per week, we would move our campsite westward. Moving days were always exciting: a new town, new people, new events, and new media coverage. The morning of moving day, we would leave the campsite we had set up a week earlier and drive about 100 kilometres to reach the spot where I had stopped the day before. I would then run 40 kilometres, and at the end of the day we would set up a new base camp 100 kilometres away.

In short, there were days when my starting point was over an hour from base camp, and others where I started running just a few kilometres from it. Our data shows that I ran 7,158 kilometres in total. With all that coming and going, travelling to attend events, the initial route to Newfoundland, and the return to Quebec after crossing Canada, the escort vehicle travelled over 60,000 kilometres in nine months.

It took me five weeks to cross Newfoundland and Labrador, the first province. Five weeks of running in the cold and the snow. Our routine had not been perfected yet, but I had the first province in the bag. From Channel-Port aux Basques, we took the ferry to North Sydney, Nova Scotia, where I resumed running.

At the start of my Canada crossing, I couldn't reach 40 kilometres each day. I was covering much more modest daily distances of 25 or 30 kilometres. I was also running all the time, taking breaks for a few minutes here and there. After a few weeks, I felt it would be more logical to divide the day into two blocks of 15 kilometres each, with a break for lunch in between. The distance was the same, but the days were much more doable for me. I recovered between the two blocks, thereby reducing my risk of injury.

Over the first eight weeks, I was able to gradually increase my daily distance to 40 kilometres. However, the third day of running in a row was always very difficult. Exhausted by the two preceding days, I struggled to reach even 30 kilometres. I had to be patient and give my body time to adapt and grow stronger. My method emerged with time, after much trial and error and by listening to my body. I respected my own limits, but always believed that they would change.

My body was like an elastic band. An elastic band can be played with forever as long as it is not stretched too far. But if it's pushed beyond its limits, it will be broken forever. The first weeks of my cross-Canada run were a warm-up. Given my limits, I did not want to run to the point of injury, which would have jeopardized the whole project and, at the same time, tainted the message, which was to show that we can all accomplish great things in spite of obstacles. I wanted to help people change their perception of diabetes so that they could see it not as a brake but as an ally, a motor, a catalyst, a springboard towards achieving their dreams.

The winter of 2014 was the worst in eastern Canada in 15 years. I ran in the snow and the cold for two months. At its worst, the temperature dipped to below -25 degrees Celsius and stayed there for a week. On several occasions, I had to run with ski goggles on to protect my eyes from frost, as the cold was piercing. The first kilometres of the day were always miserable, and, once I had warmed up, I was only tolerating the conditions that I struggled constantly against. After lunch, which we always enjoyed sheltered from the cold in the truck, it took a Herculean effort to go back out for the second half of the day.

Blizzards and heavy snowfalls were so common that, each week, we had to plan rest days around them. So as not to be late, I skipped a rest day on the day before a storm, knowing that the next day would force us to stop.

People often ask me about my motivation. I'm invited to companies to talk about my secrets and my techniques for finding, maintaining, and recovering motivation. Motivation is not something you do to get through a bad day; it's the reason you want to get through the bad day. Motivation always starts with a strong *why* ahead of you.

If you look at the origin of the word, everything makes sense. The words *motivate, motivator,* and *motivation* are all derived from the Latin *motivus,* which means "to move". This leads us to one of the most important things to understand about the topic: motivation comes once we are already in motion, not the reverse. It's action that gives rise to motivation. You want to get into shape, but don't have the motivation to start exercising? Start anyway, and the motivation will come. Never wait for motivation before acting. If you're waiting to feel motivated to start, you'll never achieve anything.

It is action that generates motivation.

When I look at photos and videos from the first months, I am the first to wonder how I did it. I wonder how I found the motivation and the energy to carry on. One day of running in -25 degrees is possible, but every day for months? That's another story. Still, when I think back to those days, my daily task did not seem so impossible. Patrick and I had vowed that no matter what happened, we would make the journey pleasant, find joy in each day, and have fun every day.

Each day was a gift, and our laughter started from the moment we woke up.

A task often seems impossible when we look at a future reality through the goggles of the today's reality. Once we've crossed the starting line, our perception changes, like how we look at our effort and abilities. The lenses through which we view the task also change. When we are in motion, things are never as bad as they seem from the outside, from the perspective of inaction. All the more reason to launch ourselves into action and believe that we will succeed.

Never judge a future reality through the lenses of the present.

It was around the 2,000-kilometre mark that I successfully ran three 40-kilometre days in a row. From that moment on, I maintained that pace for the next six months.

I lost a lot of weight at the beginning even though I was consuming thousands of calories every day, because the quality of my food was far from optimal. In hotels, without a way of cooking healthful meals, it was very difficult to eat well. And, admittedly, while Newfoundlanders are welcoming and generous hosts, their restaurants mostly offer fried foods.

Patrick, confined to the truck for two months, took up all the pounds that I was losing.

On rest days, we were often forced to stay in our hotel room due to weather conditions. The storms were rough, and the small towns where we stayed would shut down during inclement weather. Residents of the Atlantic provinces have learned over time to respect Mother Nature.

The amount of work we had to do to manage the project was colossal. We spent every rest day on our computers, occupied by all the logistics, planning, and administration of the campaign. In short, running or not, we were busy every day. We never took holidays, and every ounce of energy we had was dedicated to increasing the campaign's profile.

We updated our social media pages and shot a lot of videos to fully document our journey. We announced our supporter of the week and sent them a prize: a 15-centimetre disco ball with a note handwritten by me. We would try to have fun with whatever we were doing, knowing that to survive this crazy adventure, we would have to maintain good mental health. Attempting to stay in shape as much as possible, I went to the gym with Patrick in the evenings. Every town was a new world where we found a way to entertain ourselves.

The Seventies

I was born in September 1979, in an era of freedoms and revolutions of all kinds.

In the early 2000s, I was studying communication at the Université Laval in Quebec City. I had chosen a field that I was passionate about. While everyone else took notes, I would simply listen and let the material wash over me. I retained anything that interested me, and as for the rest, I didn't see the point in taking notes. I had the best results in courses that I deemed interesting; in others, I studied little and was satisfied with a passing mark. I wasn't lazy, I was efficient. Anyway, since I had few notes to review before exams, I could never study for long. My marks did not really matter to me. I never failed a course, but my grades were a mix of As, Bs, Cs and Ds. What mattered was that I liked what I was studying, that I found my own path, and that I made my university years memorable.

At the start of the winter of 2003, I had particular fondness for one of the lecturers who taught me. Caroline was brilliant, enthusiastic, and also very pretty. Her classes, creative and ingeniously developed, were designed to make us work. Homework for the week was always used for the next class, so you were doomed if you didn't do the work. Being forced to work to succeed, who would have thought it? Sadly, her class was the only course of its kind that I attended at university. In reality, the material was boring, but Caroline forced us to do our best, which is what made the course so interesting. It was because we were so deeply involved that the material was interesting, not the reverse.

I think we often expect passion to appear like a magic spell that will help us throw ourselves body and soul into something. Passion does not come from nothing; it's not a gift or a discovery. Investing yourself, making an effort, and becoming involved all come before developing a passion.

Passion is the result of involvement.

Many people struggle to discover their passion. Astronaut Julie Payette said, "If you don't love what you do, it may be because you don't do it well." Caroline understood this well. By forcing us to do things, she enabled us to discover a passion for the material she taught us.

In short, my passion had been set alight by the material, as well as by the messenger. I even had the brilliant idea of suggesting we go out for a drink. She told me that since I was her student, it would not be very appropriate, and that I should focus on my studies instead. At the end of the semester, immediately after the final exam, I went home and sent her a message to reiterate my request:

> Hi Caroline,
>
> Since, as of a few minutes ago, I am no longer your student, I would like to know whether you would be willing to have a drink with me.
>
> Sincerely, Sébastien

Caroline accepted my offer, and a few days later we became a couple.

I was young and reckless, filled with boundless energy, and had a head full of ideas, and nothing, absolutely nothing, seemed impossible to me. I was bordering on arrogance. I felt like I could do whatever I wanted to and succeed, but I did not have either the focus or the discipline I needed to do so.

At the time, my dreams were bigger than the man I was.

A few weeks later, Caroline and I were camping for the weekend. Late in the evening, sitting by a campfire, we wanted to reshape the world. Struck by an impulse, I suggested to Caroline that we leave to go live in California, right away, without pausing to reflect or even pack our bags. I was talking about disappearing without leaving a note, going to start a new life there. Caroline said yes. Her answer surprised me, but I couldn't back out now. We put out the fire and left. We left without telling anyone, not even our friends or families.

We drove all night and stopped to sleep at a truck stop in the early hours of the morning. All we had was a little money, our credit cards, a few clothes, and the camping gear in the car. When we woke, we were silent for a few minutes in the car, in shock from what we had done. We could still turn back. After all, we had driven only a few hours from home, our jobs, our friends, and our apartments, and we had lives waiting for us Monday morning. I asked Caroline whether she wanted to go on or go back; she said she wanted to continue. She asked me the same thing, and I answered that I was sure I also wanted to go on. I got back behind the wheel, and over the months that followed, we shared an extraordinary experience.

Years later, we confessed to one another that we hadn't wanted to continue the adventure, but we were too proud to go back on our word. We were afraid and we were both convinced that the idea was completely absurd.

We already had jobs at home. We hadn't quit, we simply never returned. We both had apartments, clothing, furniture, lives. We left all of it behind. Our roommates rented out our rooms, appropriated our furniture, and donated our clothing.

Life is so much simpler than we're led to believe. Whether you're a heart surgeon or a baker, nobody is so important or indispensable. Aside from our responsibility to our children, we can all be replaced. And since we can be replaced and can disappear tomorrow without causing waves, why live a life we don't want to live? Why not make the choices we want to and live our own lives?

I was no rookie when it came to adventures like this. In 1998, my friend Juan Pablo and I left Quebec with the idea of "travelling forever". We were both 18 and left Quebec very quickly with a grand total of $125 between us. Our plan was simple: leave the province and head west, work for a short time to earn money, then go wherever the metaphorical wind would take us. We weren't in any hurry. We dreamed of a clandestine crossing of the Pacific by boat, of spending a few years in European vineyards, and of ending up in a Buddhist monastery in Tibet.

Instead, we picked apples in the Okanagan Valley, then spent the winter at Whistler to work at a ski resort. From there, Juan Pablo headed down the American west coast, while I travelled to Japan before coming back to Vancouver for the summer of 1999. The two worldly travellers returned home about 12 months later to continue their studies. Our dream of travelling forever had quickly wilted, but I learned that you could always start a new life wherever you wanted and live it as you wanted.

My odyssey across the United States with Caroline was like a movie and it was taken in complete and absolute freedom. We stopped when we felt like it and slept in the car. The landscapes were beautiful, every second belonged to us. We were free. We did not eat like kings, but every meal was improvised in a spectacular setting. We took the time to stop and live. The destination itself was full of promises.

As far as our plans for life went, we had risked everything, and our emotions were all over the place. One minute I felt like I had made the best decision of my life. The next, I was filled with regret and worries. Who would we meet? Where and how would we find work? What kind of life would we lead? Anything was possible, and that possibility was what drove us. We were eager to discover what the future had in store for us, and we were certain we would accomplish great things.

In Denver, about halfway between Quebec and California, my insulin supply became dangerously low. I had to find a way to get more. A little embarrassed, without a prescription or even money to buy any, we decided to stop for a few days to work out a solution. Having dinner in a park one evening, an older woman noticed us. Maybe she felt that we needed help, because once we started talking, she quickly offered us hospitality.

The chance meeting was significant. We stayed with her for a week while we waited for a parcel of insulin that my friend had so generously sent by mail.

We discovered that she was a very gentle and very kind woman. Every day we spent at her home, I had the feeling that our visit was not by chance. Her son, as caring as she was, stopped by after work and told us that she had never hosted strangers before. So why us? A widow for several years, she told us the story of her life, from meeting her husband to his death. Every evening, she resumed the story where she had left off the day before. We would listen carefully, captivated, anxiously awaiting the next part. She brought out photo albums aged by the passage of time and looked at them with nostalgia, sometimes forgetting that we were there.

I felt that our presence in this woman's home was no accident, that she was looking to accomplish something or that we were bearing witness to something, as though she were closing out her account before moving on to her next destination. I had the impression of being a part of something great without really knowing what was going on. All I could do was listen and be present without trying to understand what the universe had planned. When the time came to say goodbye and continue on our path, she seemed at peace.

Arriving in California a few days later, we realized that the seventies had indeed ended. There was no commune waiting for us with open arms, food, and shelter, no jobs or even any work without a work permit, no social movements we could have joined, nothing like that at all. We did not become rich and famous by coming to California. In short, we were in a lot of trouble, and worse, we were penniless.

For the second time in my life, I had left without warning. I had left full of ambition, planning to return home only once I had shown that I could succeed. For the second time, things didn't go exactly as planned.

A question arose: Had I made the right decision?

The problem with comparing two options is that we know only a fraction of their future realities. How can two job offers, two trips, or even two partners be compared without fully knowing what the future holds? Of course, no one has a crystal ball. However, as far as imagination allows it, we must try to include what we cannot know of the future in our decision-making process. Instead of calculating what we might potentially lose because of one choice or another, we should be inspired by the possibilities their futures hold. Our decisions will then be motivated by the reality we want to create instead of being constrained by what we're afraid of compromising.

After a few days in Los Angeles, then on to San Francisco, seeing that our ambitions were not going to be achieved, Caroline and I had to change our plans. One thing was certain: the same pride that pushed us to continue down the road now prevented us from returning to Quebec.

Vancouver was about 10 hours north by car. I had spent time there in 1999, so I knew the city and I still had friends there, and Caroline and I could work there legally. The choice was obvious. We went to settle in Vancouver. With the help of a close friend who still lived there, we found an apartment and jobs that allowed us to survive. A few weeks later, our relationship ended.

I believe we were destined to undergo a similar experience and the universe brought us briefly together for that purpose, like two people who enter a room from opposite doors, walk to the middle to meet one another, exchange something, and leave again, transformed. Caroline returned to Quebec two years later, while I stayed in Vancouver for five years. The journey changed her life and mine, even though the decision was poorly planned.

In hindsight, I think we were both going through a period of self-doubt. It's an expression that means questioning yourself, which often carries a negative connotation when it should not. At the end of a romantic relationship or when we question our path or change our career, we become plagued with doubt, uncertainty, self-ignorance, and sometimes even weakness. For me, these moments are filled with excitement, exploration, and new perspectives. The secret is to look ahead to a future reality and imagine everything that could happen.

I sometimes wonder what my life would be like if I hadn't left for California. In fact, I have realized that California was just a big detour to reach Vancouver. It was there, far from home and the turmoil of my university days that I found peace. I grew up a lot there, making a few mistakes and taking a few missteps along the way, and it was during that period of my life that I grew into my dreams.

I found work in a restaurant to start. I lived humbly, learned English, and built a life there. At first glance, you could say that I was wasting time, that my place was at home, that I should have been working and preparing myself for a "real" job. I saw things differently. I was learning English, and that was the first step of my new life plan. A few years later, I started a successful career with one of the largest pharmaceutical companies in the world.

Did I make the right decision by leaving Quebec for California?

The day I got that job, I asked to meet the president of the company to discuss my plan to climb Everest. I knew nothing about "politics" in business. All I knew was that it was to him that I should speak. He received me in his office, listened to me, and told me to come back when I was ready. The company started supporting me on smaller expeditions. The marketing team and I got to know one another. My relationship with the company developed, and our values and messages became harmonized. I started doing public speaking and gained a lot of experience in mountaineering. Every year, my sponsorship money grew, and so did the mountains I was climbing. In 2008, I was ready. I had a team, an expedition, and dates, and the circumstances were favourable.

I went back to see the president of the company, this time through the right communication channels so as not to offend anyone. The meeting changed my life. I was prepared, nervous, and armed with a detailed proposal, all at the same time. However, the meeting took just a few minutes. I sat down and thanked the president for seeing me. He was sitting in his office chair, very calm. He said nothing, letting silence fill the room. I was nervous, and the silence had me fearing the worst. He took a deep breath, studied me for a long time, and, knowing why I had come, he asked, "How much do you need?"

I replied, "$100,000," and the silence resumed its dominance in the room. I was 28 years old.

He told me that he would settle everything with the finance department. He asked me one or two questions about the climb itself, and then I left the room. The marketing department received the order to make the climb the heart of its campaign for the year. I would try to become the first Canadian with type 1 diabetes to reach the summit of Everest. Globally, I would be just the third such a person in the world. I was young, presentable, ambitious, bilingual, and had a serious disease. It was a golden opportunity for the company.

While I was on Everest, a nine-person film crew was sent to Base Camp to create an ad about me. The ad was broadcast across Canada during the Beijing Olympics, an advertising investment of over $2 million. For the company, the campaign was historic. In less than a few weeks, the three-month objective of the campaign had been achieved. One of a kind, the campaign focused on inspiration rather than on the product. Parents were calling customer service to thank us, while others said they had recorded the ad to show their child who had diabetes.

I learned a lot about business and through this sponsorship, I travelled the world to give talks. None of this would have been possible without knowing a second language, learned by carrying dirty dishes in a restaurant. Seven years later, while I was in Zurich to give a TEDx talk, I learned that the president who had authorized my sponsorship had been living there for a few years. I took the opportunity to send him a short message and tell him how much he had affected my life.

So, was California a good decision?

California was a horrible decision. By leaving without warning, I disappointed a lot of people, I hurt my parents, and caused my friends to worry about me. The idea was senseless, stupid, and reckless. But what my journey has taught me is that a decision cannot itself have a negative impact on the rest of our lives.

We are often afraid of making the wrong decision, especially when we are young, as though this decision will haunt us for a long time. If THE right decision existed, we would all make the same choices, and we would all do the same thing. Every decision opens a door to a world of different opportunities, in which dozens of other decisions are constantly changing the course of our lives. Every day, we have the opportunity to change the path we're on. Whatever the setbacks and mistakes, we always find many doors along the way, leading to our full realization.

We spend our lives making decisions, but above all trying to make the right decisions. Which university to choose? Which field to study? Should I follow my passion and become a painter at the risk of living in a precarious financial situation, or should I study administration and find a less interesting job to subsist and meet the needs of my family? Should I stay here or accept a job offer at the other end of the world? Should I spend the rest of my days with the same person, or seek new experiences?

My journey is not a straight line. I've accomplished great things, taken several detours, taken many steps backward, and made many mistakes. People say that everything happens for a reason. That's often true, but I've also learned that nothing is pointless. Every decision, every meeting, every event, every life lesson, every setback, and every success is part of the foundation of the next adventure and enriches it even more.

Today, I never compare more than two choices when trying to make the right decision. My choices are not a good-or-bad binary: I consider two valid options and choose the one that gives me the greater opportunity for growth based on my goals.

Each decision leads to a result, which is neither good nor bad, just different. Different meetings, different opportunities, a different life. When decisions are motivated by a sincere desire to follow our path, there are no disappointments, just discoveries.

Our choices change, too. They should change. We all experience what we call periods of self-doubt a few times over the course of our lives. The more we love our work, the more we lead a life we want to live, the more we wonder what kind of legacy we're leaving behind. Are we happy? Are we leading the life we imagined when we were younger? Some find their lives too complicated and dream of abandoning everything to sell fruit smoothies on a beach in Bali. For others, it's the exact opposite: life is too simple. After years of going in circles, they realize the extent of their talents and reinvent their careers.

What we must understand is that our past choices were neither good nor bad. We make decisions based on what we know and the information we have at the time. It's like going to buy an ice cream cone at the neighbourhood ice cream parlour. With a choice of three flavours (vanilla, chocolate, or Neapolitan) you choose the one you like best. For years, whenever you get to the counter, without even thinking about it, you ask for the same flavour. For years, our career, the town where we live, the significance of our relationships, our values, and our priorities can be completely comfortable. But one day, 24 flavours are available.

Opportunities we never even knew about are now available to us. They do not make our old choices bad, they simply offer new opportunities to choose something else. These opportunities take every form: a career you never considered, an encounter that opens you to values you find more agreeable, a chance to become self-employed, a relationship that ends, a relationship that begins.

**The range of choices available to us is not static.
It is constantly expanding and changing.**

What you must remember is that we are not restricted to our lives as they are or to the choices we made five or 10 years ago. That said, if vanilla ice cream is still your favourite despite all the new flavours, there's nothing wrong with sticking with that choice! Our only duty to ourselves is to try to make choices that promote our growth. Making new personal and professional choices does not make us indecisive, turncoats, or opportunists. What worked for us 10 years ago does not necessarily still work today. We can and should allow ourselves the right to change our minds, as heart-wrenching as it can sometimes be.

The War Amps Team

I scaled Everest alongside some extraordinary men. We were five climbers accompanied by two Canadian guides and 15 Sherpa. In fact, without the aid of the Sherpa people, almost no ascension would be possible. Only a small handful of climbers are capable of accomplishing the feat without support, and from time to time, another team attempts it. The Sherpa are a good, generous, humble, and hardworking people, and they are the force that makes the summit possible for the rest of us. They allow us onto their mountain and lead us to the summit because they want to. I'm reminded of Then Dorjee Sherpa, a young and fascinating man in whose company I achieved the Mount Everest climb. Sadly, he was killed in an avalanche on that mountain a few years later.

I was 28 years old when I climbed Mount Everest. I was one of the youngest people in the world to attempt the climb, with my head full of dreams, and I was determined to succeed and do anything to reach the summit. I prepared myself for years. I would be lying if I said that I wasn't attracted to the glory of Everest at the start, because I was, extremely so. I was young, immature, and motivated by different reasons, external to myself, that pushed me to do what I had to do to reach my goal. Over the years, especially considering my disease, my motivation shifted towards the message I wanted to send and the impact I wanted it to have.

One day, after giving a talk, a 10-year-old child asked me whether I thought I would have scaled Everest if I didn't have diabetes. It was a difficult question to answer. After having reflected upon it, I think the answer is yes. However, I also think that I might not have reached the summit, or at least that my ascension would not have brought so much joy.

I had a dream, and diabetes gave it a reason and meaning. The condition allowed me to focus the intention behind my actions on others instead of on myself. Through my actions, I wanted to show that if someone with type 1 diabetes could reach the summit of Everest, then anyone's dream, big or small, was possible.

Four fascinating and inspiring men climbed alongside me during the expedition: Rob Hill, Wayne Browning, Erik Bjarnason, and Darrell Ainscough. I had the privilege of meeting them in the years before Everest, since we used the same logistics company to plan our expeditions and mountain-climbing training. The owner put us in contact with one another, knowing that we all shared the same ultimate goal. These men became my teammates, friends, and guides.

Rob was 38 years old when we climbed Everest in 2008. He has Crohn's disease. A great inspiration for those with this condition, he has also successfully scaled the seven highest peaks in the world. Rob had to leave us early on because of complications caused by his condition. Two years later, he returned for a second try and became the first person with Crohn's disease to scale Mount Everest.

Erik is a firefighter and is in love with mountain climbing. In 2005, he lost almost all his fingers on Mount Logan during a climb that became a nightmare. Lost on the mountain, their tent buffeted by the wind, and trapped in a violent storm, he and his team huddled in the snow and waited for death. Rescue teams miraculously found them, but the cold took Erik's fingers in the process. The miracle survivors received considerable media attention, and what Erik said from his hospital bed is a testament to his wisdom, his strength, and his greatness. "I may have lost my fingers, but I can still hold my children in my arms."

Wayne was my tentmate. He was always in a cheery mood. He was in great physical shape and a seasoned climber. I loved his calm and his banter. He was responsible for carrying the emergency equipment for my diabetes. If I were to become severely hypoglycemic, he was responsible for giving me an injection of glucagon, which would save my life. He was 71 years old at the time.

Wayne did not reach the summit. Halfway into the expedition, exhausted, he told me, "I came here to have fun. I have millions in the bank, and since I'm not having fun anymore, I'm going to go home and have some fun!" And that's just what he did. Throughout the expedition, Wayne taught me that the lessons were not waiting at the summit, but were spread out across the mountain.

Darrell was in good health, but we still took him onto our team.

Upon arrival at Base Camp in early April, each team sets up its tents: personal tents for climbers, the cooking tent, the shower tent, and the toilet tent. Considerable efforts are made to minimize the human impact, and a barrel is installed under the toilet tent so that even human waste does not pollute the environment.

Base Camp is a fascinating international village. Approximately 200 climbers of about 30 different nationalities meet up every year. Tents of many colours are pitched on the ice to create a multicoloured community. At night, headlamps hanging in the tents create a wondrous light show. The metallic clangs of pots and the continuous laughter of the celebrating Sherpa fill the emptiness. When the stars are out, nighttime is often the most beautiful time of day. The moon illuminates the sleepless giants, and the stars seem so close. Every breath of the thin air at that altitude is a lesson in humility. Emotionally, I switched often between anxiety and excitement, without any warning before a switch happened, and without any idea of how long the new emotion would take hold for.

Intrigued by our unusual climbing team, other climbers visited our campsite, curious and filled with questions. *Aren't you afraid?* Some of the more experienced climbers doubted our chances of success, while others outright suggested that we were a danger on the mountain. Still, I never would have made the climb with anyone else. Our team was strong. The secret ingredient? Our vulnerability. Only when we accept our vulnerability can we become strong.

Being strong means recognizing your vulnerability.

Imagine what our respective conditions imposed upon us. Imagine the impact of our weaknesses on our training. At each period of training, each of us had to arrive with perfect planning and preparation. Nothing could be left to chance. Each of us had to prove to the rest of the team that we were fully prepared and armed with several contingency plans. Our conditions forced each of us to think, improve, and practice several systems and concepts that would be essential on the mountain. In a society that continuously pushes us to go higher, go faster, be more beautiful, be richer, and become more successful, we can be tempted to hide our vulnerabilities. However, it's thanks to this vulnerability, and especially from welcoming it, that we become strong.

Not surprisingly, there are many parallels with a company. Think about our system of communication. Think about how we had to share knowledge for the common good and for the success and safety of the team. Individual glory was always set aside. The team's mission was more important than any individual success.

For a team to succeed, the mission must be
more important than individual success.

In sport, as in business, this rule is the most important element in creating a winning team. A strong mission should be the top priority. The team members must be dedicated to it, must believe in it, must be convinced that the mission is important. The mission itself increases everyone's commitment, which in turn increases the performance of each person. It's the mission that lifts up individuals.

We had an unusual climbing team. It was our individual weaknesses that bonded us together. Everyone knew that at one time or another they would depend on the team, and that other times would be their chance to shine. Our roles would have to be exchanged, always working towards completing our mission and swallowing our pride. We must all be leaders, we must all help others become better, and never fall into the trap of competitiveness. We all understood that when one candle lights another, it loses nothing, but the whole room becomes much brighter. Our team was a real collaborative laboratory, a fascinating experiment on developing a strong team spirit. Several lessons learned can in fact be applied to the corporate world and to any kind of organization.

Trust is earned, not given. We had rubbed shoulders for years in the mountains. We had built the bonds of trust that we would need to tackle Everest together. Each person's humility was tested and confirmed by the team. At every training session, our level of commitment was observed by the others. Each person's strengths and weaknesses had to be known by all. We had to learn to accept our limitations and let the team take over when we needed to gather our strength.

The result was magnificent. Individually, our failings, our innate defects, and our disabilities were weaknesses. Together, our many individual weaknesses turned into a great collective strength.

> The strength of a sports team or a work team is its ability to transform several distinct elements, strengths, and weaknesses into a single unit.

Strengths are not added together, they are multiplied. Individual weaknesses are subtracted, swallowed, and compensated by the power of the newly created unit.

The Sahara

I was fascinated by this challenge from the moment I first heard about it. It was a 250-kilometre race over five days, in almost complete self-sufficiency, in the Sahara Desert. It was 250 kilometres of running in the sand in sweltering temperatures that hovered between 40 and 45 degrees Celsius. *Time* Magazine designated the Sahara race one of the 10 most difficult endurance competitions in the world. I was on the starting line in the fall of 2012.

From Everest to the Sahara. There was something very enticing about it. Like my other starting lines, my instincts told me to trust in my path, that the answers would appear once I was there. I was familiar with the cold, chasms, and high altitudes. This time, the environment would be completely different: extreme heat, sand, and an endurance race. The questions I was asking myself were the same as the ones that companies ask in periods of major change. How do I maintain performance and keep pace in a changing environment? What do I do to adapt and stay ahead in this new world? Where to begin? How can acquired expertise be used to apply to a different context? How do I motivate the team and make sure everyone has a desire to change?

The Sahara did not disappoint me. Nowadays, my talk on change management, transformation, and corporate agility is the one I give the most often. Here is the key message of that talk: change is not an action, it is a culture. It is not an event, it is a process. You must sometimes forget the summit and be in love with the process.

In our grandparents' time, companies had been doing the same thing for decades. Then their world was turned upside down and panic arose, because companies had to quickly adapt to the change by adopting new technology or changing their methods. They adapted to change, but really, they reacted to change. Change was not proactive, quite the contrary: it was reactive. They surrendered as if they were taking cough syrup: only when it hurts. Once the storm passed, and if the company had survived, it rested on its success until the next upheaval.

Firstly, when we adapt to change, it's usually a sign that we've already lost the war. It's a sign that the competitor is dictating the pace. What's more, these days, everything is constantly changing: the climate, consumer habits, the market, technology, culture, competition, laws, and so on. The saying "adapt to change" is itself outdated. In business, we should instead be talking about agility.

Agility in business is a culture. It's a muscle that must be trained every day by integrating change into every meeting, into every project, and at every level of the company.

Once change becomes part of the company's identity, culture, and DNA, it becomes agile. It becomes capable of responding more quickly and more easily to changes in the industry and, even better, of anticipating them. It can change its processes more quickly when they are not working. It can adopt new technology more easily or quickly change how it operates when the market turns.

By becoming agile, the company stops reacting to change and starts using it to stand out and earn more. The agile company makes change a weapon and a competitive advantage.

Change is not an action.
It is a culture.

The more we innovate, the more likely we are to fail. Some things will not work as planned, projects will not all go smoothly. That's normal and desirable. If we've taken care to create an environment where everyone can fail with success, in a climate that encourages growth, the company will move forward.

After several years on snowy mountaintops, I was ready for a change. I had a deep conviction that this new setting would be rich with new lessons to be learned. The years I spent doing triathlons helped me get into excellent physical shape and develop great endurance. I learned a lot about sports nutrition, as well as training and recovery techniques. I spent much of 2012 preparing for my last triathlon, then concentrated my efforts on the Sahara Race. Training for ultramarathons does not require Herculean effort. In any case, that was my perspective. Obviously, the task would have seemed impossible a few years earlier. One step at a time, the things I believed possible, my tolerance to effort, and my physical endurance had been transformed.

Training for an ultra-marathon is fairly simple. Recovery is half the battle. You don't run every day. In fact, three or four runs per week to the tune of 15 or 20 kilometres each run is enough. Very little training in speed is required. Instead, the body is preparing to run slowly over very long distances. A long run of 30, 40, or 50 kilometres should also be taken each week. One weekend day, we trot easily along, without too much suffering, and enjoy the scenery.

The rest of the time, training takes other shapes: special attention is given to nutrition and sleep, stretching and strengthening exercises, preparing equipment and nutrition for long runs, cutting down on alcohol, and more. This is a key part of training, and success with these less visible aspects multiplies the value of all the hard-won kilometres.

From Montreal, I arrived in Cairo, Egypt's capital, where 134 participants from 30 different countries were gathering in the same hotel. The atmosphere was reminiscent of Everest Base Camp, with people from all over the world sharing the same goal, anxious, excited, and inspired by different motivations.

We had all arrived a few days before the race was to begin to absorb the jet lag and attend various logistical and safety meetings.

At one of these meetings, each participant had to show their equipment and food supply to the officials. We had been sent a list of mandatory items months in advance, and the slightest omission could disqualify us. The list included a minimum of 15,000 calories for the whole five days of the competition. With a daily average of 5,000 to 7,000 calories, depending on the participant, this minimum amount was far from a luxury. Most participants had opted for a reserve well beyond the minimum. Conscious of how their bag's weight will impact performance, those aspiring to be in the top 20 spots, of which I was one, chose to carry a much more restricted larder. Everyone was trying to find the perfect formula to balance performance, load, and comfort. Good comfort and proper nutrition result in faster recovery and better next-day performance. However, a heavier bag slows even the most physically fit. Since we're all different, there was no right or wrong way to prepare. Each person had to find their own optimal formula. Add a competitive atmosphere and individuals who take pleasure in effort and pain, and the Sahara Race becomes an incredible performance laboratory.

Peak performance is a topic that I discuss often. If you ask Olympic medalists to replicate their performance one month after winning their medal, they won't be able to do it. The body cannot maintain the same perfect performance forever. Athletes push their bodies to the edge of their abilities for a short moment, such as at the Olympic Games or another major competition, and then rest before preparing for the next one. Peak performance involves synchronizing your best performance with the moment it matters the most.

I once observed a workshop for Olympic athletes in which the instructor asked the participants: what are you most afraid of about the Olympic Games you're preparing for? The answers were unanimous. The greatest fear of those athletes was that they would suddenly be unable to accomplish the task they had mastered when the time came.

> Peak performance does not
> mean being good forever.
> It means being unbeatable when
> it matters the most.

Adapt this to your reality. If, like the Olympic athlete, I could only meet an important client once every four years, how would I prepare myself? That's what peak performance is. You don't have to be at the top of your form every moment of every day. Preparation requires thoroughness, flexibility, and humility. Sometimes it also requires us to stop and take a step back to better understand how to progress. It requires us to apply ourselves, to learn, and to adapt so that, when we need it, we are unbeatable.

At work and at home, we are always asked for more. Often, the pressure comes from ourselves. Company objectives for sales, profitability, and growth are increasingly demanding. The pressure to achieve them is high, and the environment is increasingly competitive. In short, everything is always getting more difficult. By dissecting maximum performance and realizing that it does not mean being permanently at the top of your abilities, you will have an important realization: balance and performance can coexist. In fact, they must coexist, because each is an essential ingredient to the other. Without balance, without a fulfilling personal life, you will never excel at work, and the opposite is equally true. Without professional success, it is difficult to take trips. And without vacations, God knows that you are not pleasant to be around.

Finding the balance between comfort and performance is an art, both in the desert and in our professional and personal lives. For how long does the desire to succeed justify sacrifice? How do you find the balance between living in the moment and planning for the future? Take my present reality, for example. You're reading this book months or even years after I've written it. But as I write it now, I'm sitting at my desk working on the manuscript. It's sunny out, and today is a holiday. The window of my office overlooks the pool at the complex where I live. Should I write the whole day in the hope that my book will bring success, or should I head down to the pool with a cocktail to enjoy life? Who knows, I could get hit by a bus tomorrow morning! My journey has taught me many things, but I have no answer to this thought. People often say that life is short. While I don't disagree with this assertion, I also don't agree with it. I have not hit 40 yet. If a bus hit me tomorrow morning, if a loved one were to hold me in their arms a few seconds before I shut my eyes, I would say that my life had been extraordinary.

Life is not long, and it's fragile, but I'm not sure that it is so short, either. I usually find that those who think life is short are those who feel left behind. Personally, it's not the length that matters, but the value.

Live as if each day is your last. You don't have to agree, but to me, this expression has no meaning and doesn't inspire me. I even find it childish. If I knew I would die tomorrow, I'm not sure that I would want to dance and travel around the world! Disagree? Perhaps a visit to a palliative care residence would be educational. Those people could die tomorrow, and the last I heard, they aren't having a party.

I won't die tomorrow. I want to live and plan for the future. I want to enjoy today while doing everything I can to improve my lot and that of my loved ones. I want to create wealth and spend a lot to have as many experiences as possible. I live by enjoying each day, regardless of the number of days I have left. I don't live as though today is my last day. I live as though I will die soon.

If you don't want to change your life, your actions, or your job, regardless of when the end will be, whether it's tomorrow or in 60 years, that's a sign that you're living well.

The race through the Sahara is conducted in almost complete self-sufficiency. Participants are supplied with water and tents, nothing more. We carry everything else on our shoulders for the whole race: food, equipment, and everything else. The backpack gets lighter every day as our food reserves decrease.

For an entire week, our whole lives were based on our backpacks. Besides the mandatory supplies, each participant could choose the size of bag and what went into it. Since the tents were pitched on the sand, I decided not to bring a mattress. Every gram mattered, and I thought that the sand would be soft enough for me to sleep comfortably without a mat. This was probably my biggest mistake. Each night, the sand became packed and hard under my weight. The ground was irregular and extremely uncomfortable, to the point that my recovery was severely affected.

Our backpacks were metaphors. Like in our professional and personal lives, it's not the superfluous that bothers us. What we always regret the most is what is likely to hurt us the most, it's those things we choose not to bring with us. Life allows us a limited number of choices. What type of relationships and values do we choose to fill it with?

Sometimes, others invite themselves into our bags, before we can decide whether to give them a place or not. Since space is limited, what we choose to put in is crucial. If we put in the wrong objectives, wrong people, or wrong values, we will run out of space for what really matters.

Is life long or short? I cannot answer this question. But like the Sahara Race, it does have an end. All the time spent carrying the wrong things in your bag is wasted time, lost forever. Pay attention to what you put in the backpack of your life, because no one else will carry it for you. A bag that is too heavy, filled with bad things, hurts your shoulders and is difficult to carry.

Conscious of the weight of my bag, I chose a very small backpack. In the weeks preceding the race, I spent many hours trying to make everything fit in the bag. I tried every possible arrangement, but nothing worked. It was like a 3D puzzle that I was unable to solve until I decided to remove a few items.

Why fight with the zipper your whole life when you can simply remove something from the bag?

Our bag is never too small. It's just that sometimes we put the wrong things into it.

Sahara Race, Day 1

From day one, I was struck by the vastness of the desert. I had been similarly struck by the immensity of the mountains in Nepal a few years earlier. This time around, it was the vastness of the empty space and its power that impressed me. The horizon was both empty and beautiful.

Like in any endurance competition, some participants were not athletes. Some of them knew this and had no intention of running. They just wanted to walk the distance and discover the Sahara this way. Others had not grasped the magnitude of the challenge. It goes without saying that they did not finish the race. It is usually at this point that a touching and inspiring story of determination is told, a story of an underdog, of a person who starts off as a loser and finishes victoriously ahead of the favoured winners, or who just manages to finish, but inspires us all through a message of hope. Not in this case. Pride, willpower, and perseverance cannot replace hundreds of hours of training.

Ambition without work is naivety.

Among participants, we had a few days to share our aspirations about what we wanted to achieve. Generally, the strongest competition is yourself. Apart from one or two exceptions, we were all experiencing the desert for the first time. Another striking realization: we all shared the same fear, that of the unknown. We shared it, but above all, it brought us together. The years after Everest had come one after the other. I participated in a few triathlons; the first had been terrifying, but the fright faded after a few competitions. However, for the first time in years, I felt that fear once again. Pushed by that fear, my training was much more rigorous. I read everything I could find on the Sahara Race, tested all my equipment, and carefully planned my meals and my hydration strategy.

I also noticed that many competitors seemed to lead successful lives. Most of them were business people from small or large companies, some directors, some professionals. It was not just our passion for running and adventure that had brought us together. I think the race and adventure were simply vehicles through which we were expressing our desire for growth. This quest was inevitably one of discomfort and the unknown. Despite that, the atmosphere was calm, cheery, and relaxed. Fear manifested itself through an eagerness to live this experience and discover what it had to offer.

The race is relatively simple: five timed events in five days, the first four being approximately 40 kilometres each, ending with a fifth stage of 87 kilometres. Departure began at seven o'clock each morning. Water refill stations were set up at every 10 kilometres. Each participant should be able to carry three litres of water. The water stations also acted as checkpoints where medical staff and logistics officials were stationed. Doctors and nurses were there to ask questions, provide care, and give permission to each participant to continue the race.

In extreme heat, water consumption is never the problem. What becomes crucial is ingesting electrolytes. Given the large amounts of sodium and minerals that leave the body when you sweat, it's critical that essential electrolytes are added to your water. Drinking too much water and not enough electrolytes when you sweat a lot for many hours can be very dangerous. Obviously, you have nothing to fear on a long Sunday run, even in hot weather. But in conditions like those found in the Sahara, electrolytes are vital. A laminated card was attached to the backpack of each runner, with a box for each water station passed every day. Staff assigned to logistics punched these cards religiously each time we filled our bottles. The card served as a way to carefully monitor our water and electrolyte consumption.

This race does not involve orienteering, so the runners do not have to find their way themselves. Each morning, organizers mark the next leg of the race with small pink flags in the sand. Runners simply follow these flags over 40 kilometres, and the day is done. It's easier said than done, of course, and vigilance is always required. Set at every 50 metres, the 30-centimetre-high-pink flags can easily blend into their surroundings. The rule is simple: always find the next flag before continuing onward; if you cannot see a flag, stop immediately and go back to find the next flag before moving on.

The stages were timed to maintain a general classification. Thinking back to my first steps, a few minutes after the starting signal was launched on day one, I realized that I had no idea what was coming, or what this week had in store for us. This is often true of most great experiences and transition periods.

Most of the 250 kilometres is sand, except for a few sections on gravel. For the first hours of the first day, we try a little of everything, we check our markers, and we try to find our rhythm. I settled into 20th position and calmly followed the footprints left by the faster competitors.

I love running in winter. I love the feeling of the cold and, dressed in appropriate clothing, low temperatures never worried me. Ironically, snow and the unstable surfaces it causes perfectly reproduce the conditions of the terrain in the Sahara. In the snow, when footprints are left ahead of you, your instinct is to follow them exactly. Trampled snow is more compact, harder, and therefore provides an easier path to run. In the desert, I followed the same instinct to run in the footprints that runners had left behind. Bad idea.

In some places, the sun bakes the sand to make a tough crust. Once the crust is broken by the faster runners, their footprints expose more crumbly sand, which is more difficult to run on. After a few minutes spent running in the footprints of others, I noticed that the path widened instead of looking like a trail. I realized that runners were seeking the crust, the harder sand where no one had stepped, which was more effective for running. Similarly, following your own path is always the fastest and best way to developing your full potential.

It took just a few hours for the Sahara to impose its rules and show us it was the boss. We had all arrived well-rested, well-fed, fully trained, and in pursuit of specific objectives. We had all underestimated the magnitude of the task. Having just begun, with just a few kilometres behind us and another five days of running ahead, all our objectives were vaporized. Each step was difficult, our bags bruised our shoulders. The heat was unbearable, each person progressed more slowly than they expected, and even those in the best shape had to alternate between walking and running. I wondered how I would even survive the first day.

In short, after having run barely a dozen kilometres, surviving and finishing the race was all we wanted. The desert quickly tamed us, and the lesson in humility was intense. It's fascinating to see that we all received the same lesson, almost simultaneously and as quickly as the next. As though the desert were trying to show us something, we went from being competitors to being teammates.

What an incredible experience it was to be forced to look for something other than what we thought we would find! The futile quest for a good time was overshadowed; the Sahara had much greater things to offer.

In these conditions, the fastest racers finished each 40-kilometre leg in about five hours. I needed to run six or seven hours to stay roughly in roughly 20th place. From 9 or 10 a.m., the sun blazed down upon us. Water plays the important role in hydration, of course, but it also plays an essential role in cooling us down. When undergoing intense physical effort, we are naturally inclined towards cold water, since it helps maintain body temperature at the right level.

In the desert, the temperature rose to between 40 and 45 degrees Celsius every day. Our bodies are set to operate at 37 degrees. Our water bottles were attached to the front of our backpacks, and were therefore not protected from the sun, so the water inside quickly rose to the ambient temperature.

Imagine you were running in the desert, thirsty, and completely out of breath, and the only thing you had to drink was hot water. The hot water worsens your situation by warming your body even more, which means you end up sweating out the water without benefiting from it.

As the day progressed, the race became even tougher. By late morning, the sand had already collected a lot of heat. The air became hot, searing the lungs in moments, making any effort almost impossible. The heat was intolerable, and the effort needed to run in these conditions with a still fully loaded backpack was titanic.

On crossing the first finish line, I felt as if I could not have taken another step. Most of the runners felt the same way. That night, and for the rest of the week, a big question drove much of our conversation: if we were struggling to finish each day, how would we survive the fifth and final stage of 87 kilometres?

Sahara Race, Day 2

I started the second day at the rear of the group, still sore from the first day. The route was long, and keeping my energy stores in check was my main concern. The beginning of the day was rather difficult. Slowly but surely, I climbed the ranks to finish in 19th place. The second day was easier than the first.

You get used to it and orient yourself more easily, the terrain becomes more familiar, and your fear of the unknown fades.

By starting towards the rear of the group, I was able to establish and achieve several small goals over the course of the day.

With a hundred competitors to pass ahead of me, my attention was completely diverted from the finish line. I focused on the task at hand: pass the person ahead of me. The finish line was far, intimidating, and difficult to imagine. The runner ahead of me was very real, quite tangible, and never too far away. With a little effort, passing someone was always possible.

> The more you divide a task into small and
> realistic steps, the easier it is to achieve them.

More than that, each time you pass someone and each step you take, however small, you develop the conviction and the profound feeling that you are capable, competent, and adequate, that you can succeed, that you have the right to succeed, and that you deserve to succeed. By dividing the task into as many steps as possible, we multiply our opportunities for success and safe learning. The length of the step does not matter. What matters is what it means and what transformation it launches. The common denominator among those who succeed is not talent, but the belief that they can succeed.

The good news is that belief in your ability to succeed is something that you acquire, learn, develop, maintain, and refine—and something you lose if you do not maintain it. Like everything else, it takes practice to excel. All my life, I was told I had to practise to achieve success. One day, I realized that you must also practise succeeding. The difference is subtle, but incredibly important. Practising to succeed is an intriguing concept, isn't it?

We practise a sport or a hobby to improve. Why not practise to succeed, and therefore succeed more easily? The main obstacles to success are often our own beliefs and doubts. Many people, often without even realizing it, don't grant themselves the right to succeed. They believe that success is for others, that they do not deserve it. Most people believe that they have granted themselves the right to succeed, but in reality, few have a sincere and profound belief that they really deserve it. Who would dare say in public that they don't have the right to succeed or that they don't deserve it? Almost no one.

Imagine you are a multimillionaire. Imagine finishing a marathon in first place. Imagine living in a luxurious residence in an upscale neighbourhood. Imagine yourself at the head of the company you work for now. How do you feel?

Some will be at ease. Others, even if they claim they want to succeed, will have a bout of impostor syndrome simply from imagining themselves at the top. I've talked a lot about the importance of the first step. Often this first step is internal, a first step towards yourself.

If you do not take the first step towards yourself,
the first step towards your goal will be useless.

We watch others succeed. Do I deserve to win? Do I have the right to win, to become accomplished? Changing your beliefs takes time, patience, and above all, practice. To succeed, you must familiarize yourself with the recipe and flavour of success. You must know how to use it, understand its mechanisms, and become comfortable in its world. What I mean is success in the broad sense, be it financial, academic, romantic, or personal. Success must be learned! Practising to succeed, developing a deep conviction that I could succeed and that I deserved to succeed is what I was unconsciously doing at the start of my second day behind everyone in the Sahara. I finished 19th and, by passing more than 100 people that day, I reached 100 goals. I succeeded a hundred times and I developed the feeling that I was capable of winning.

With this change in my beliefs, day three was the stage on which I gave my best performance in the desert. I took risks and chose a different strategy that I believed in, confident that I was competent, that I was physically capable, and that I could succeed.

Sahara Race, Day 3

Each morning was hard, and the third morning was no exception. The first steps were always stiff, and I always wondered how I would manage. The muscle tension in my pelvis was so intense that my spine arched when I lay on my back. My weight was plummeting, recovery was almost impossible, and hunger was a constant presence. I somehow resisted the temptation to use up food rations earmarked for the following days.

With every passing day, my body's strength faded, but my spirit picked up the slack. Each new day seemed a little less intimidating. We knew that the third day would be extremely difficult, that we would doubt ourselves at times, but that we would eventually see the finish line. Up to now, I had been starting each day very slowly to ensure I properly managed what energy I had. On the third day, I completely changed my strategy; rather than starting off slow, I kicked off with a roar.

Bolstered by my experience of the day before, it was the conviction that I could succeed that made all the difference. I tried to take advantage of the cooler temperatures and lower sun of the first two hours. I was taking a risk, I was trying something new. I took this risk in good humour and as an experiment, curious about the result, open to failure, but confident in my abilities. I gave myself permission to fail without letting it impact my confidence. I also gave myself the right to succeed by relying on my observations and the expertise I had acquired in the preceding days.

I had noticed that by 10 or 11 o'clock, the heat became so overwhelming that all participants slowed their pace considerably. No matter how much energy remained, the sun reduced us to jogging at a very slow pace or to outright walking. So from that time on, the rankings changed very little; any major changes took place at the beginning of the day.

My game plan was twofold: empty my energy tank to gain the greatest possible lead and settle into the best position I could reach before the heat took over, then protect my position and survive until the finish line.

The confidence I had built up in day two helped me to start at the head of the pack on day three and feel I belonged there. I practised to succeed. I finished the third stage of the Sahara Race in ninth place, surrounded by some of the best athletes in the world.

Jack Poisson

If you draw a line from St. John's in Newfoundland and Labrador, to Vancouver, British Columbia, the path swings northwest at Montreal, passes through Ottawa, then crosses north of the Great Lakes. The problem with this route is that it skips Toronto and its surrounding region, where one third of the country's population lives. The goal of Run Across Canada was to see as many people as possible and, at the same time, to have the widest possible impact. Of course, this could only be achieved through a lot of media coverage, so hitting Toronto on the route was essential. Early on in the project, I made the decision to lengthen the journey to go through this metropolis. I therefore ran across Canada in two continuous lines: from St. John's, Newfoundland and Labrador, to Windsor, Ontario, and from Sault Ste. Marie, Ontario, to Vancouver, British Columbia.

From Windsor, we drove the truck and trailer through the United States to pick up the route in Sault Ste. Marie. Since the latter is almost due north of the former, and since I was lengthening my journey to see even more people, this choice felt honest and reasonable to me.

In Windsor in June 2014, when I was approaching the halfway mark, I met Jack Poisson, a 10-year-old with type 1 diabetes. He and his family attended an evening hosted by one of my sponsors. Jack dreamed of running across Ontario to raise money for diabetes research. He had stars in his eyes, a little sister that was as charming as she was energetic, and absolutely exceptional parents.

Often in great adventures, there's a great moment, a heart-warming event, an episode that defines the entire adventure and that you remember forever. For me, that moment was meeting Jack.

A few days after that memorable evening, the Poisson family surprised me on the road while I was coming up on the last kilometre in Windsor. My arrival in the city marked the halfway point of my journey. It was a major milestone in my route, my first major victory. I had run halfway across Canada, and, step by step, my dream was becoming a reality. The project was gaining popularity, and thousands of people were following my journey in the media. Windsor also marked the end of a stage in another way. The next segment of the campaign would be completely different, more psychologically difficult, and more physically demanding.

Jack ran with me for the last seven kilometres of the first segment at an impressive pace. We celebrated that finish line with a few other families who had come out for the occasion. The next day, the Poisson family sent Patrick and me an invitation to their family barbecue, and we would not have dreamed of refusing.

We quickly bonded with the Poisson family. Jack talked to us as if our friendship was a thousand years old, and we talked as if we were the same age. We each had great admiration for the other. I saw myself at his age in him, and he saw himself in me too, I think. There were a few times when I had a very strong impression of seeing a younger version of myself, disguised as a stranger and conveying an important message. Then, since all good things must come to an end, it sadly came time to say goodbye.

A few days later, I was beginning the second part of my crossing, which stretched 1,400 kilometres from Sault Ste. Marie to Winnipeg in Manitoba. Nearly two months of running in the middle of nowhere awaited me, far and away the most difficult part of the journey.

It was a cloudy afternoon, and I had barely left Sault Ste. Marie when Patrick drove up alongside me in the truck. It was an unusual gesture, and the passenger-side window was rolled down. Then I heard Jack's voice.

When he got home from school, Jack decided to give us a call. He wanted to make sure that I was staying in shape, that I was eating well, and that Patrick was not too bored. Jack called us every week for the rest of the journey. What was most touching about it was that part of his reason for phoning us was to find out where we were, but mostly it was to make sure that we were doing well.

Patrick often put the call on speaker phone, and for a few minutes I would run alongside the truck while we spoke with Jack. Those moments we spent talking together were wonderful! We spoke about everything and nothing, about the sports Jack played, public speaking he had begun to do, and his involvement in causes fighting diabetes.

At our first meeting in Windsor, Jack had offered me a box full of loose change, money which he had collected for diabetes research, but which he had instead decided to give me to support my campaign.

That box is in my bookcase to this day, the currency still inside. For me, it's a symbol of generosity, self-sacrifice, and purity. On his birthday a few months later, when I was still running, Jack's family organized a party with his friends, like usual, but Jack asked all his friends to make a donation to my campaign instead of bringing gifts.

Five months later, Jack and his family travelled to Vancouver to be there for my arrival. In fact, by planning with Patrick and the arrival production team, they plotted to surprise me. The day before my final marathon, I attended a production meeting with 15 other people. Jack burst into the room, taking me completely by surprise and triggering a tsunami of emotion. I was incredibly moved. The next morning, we ran the last kilometres together.

A few days later, I was at a party organized to honour friends, collaborators, and sponsors of the campaign. Jack seemed concerned about something all night, and when it came time to go, his parents found him crying. This time, it really was the end. Jack was worried we would never see each other again, that our paths would never cross again. That night, it was actually very difficult to say goodbye. It was the end of something, and it was heartbreaking for everyone.

The Poisson family are among some of my closest friends today. Two years after the campaign, I was in Vancouver to give a talk on purpose driven leadership. Alerted by social media that I was in town, Jack's mother phoned me. It just so happened that the Poisson family was in Vancouver for a wedding! Jack intended to go to the beach where the campaign had ended to recall some memories. With his parents' help, it was my turn to surprise Jack.

Dunes

The Sahara Race is a well-organized event. Registered months in advance, participants undergo a long preparatory phase. During the months before the event, organizers send regular communications on the logistics of the race, mandatory equipment, and rules, as well as educational articles about training and nutrition for appropriate preparation. Medical tests and a doctor's approval are required to confirm your registration. Nothing is left to chance, and the organizers do everything they can to make sure the event is both safe and fun.

Each participant must carry a reasonably well-packed first aid kit, much of which is dedicated to treating blisters. There are two kinds of blisters: the pretty ones, and the less pretty ones. All it takes is an Internet search for the words "blisters", "feet", and "Sahara Race" to understand the severity of the injuries some athletes suffer in this race. They aren't the small, dime-sized blisters, which could almost be called cute, filled with a transparent liquid. These are severe blisters that make the whole foot seem like it's rotting, infected, and red and blue, and your nails might even fall off.

I was training as much as possible. I was building up my maximum range with a full backpack on my shoulders, and I frequently tested my nutrition strategy to improve it. When I first saw those pictures of bruised and blistered feet, I had to accept the truth: regardless of your degree of physical fitness, anyone who develops such severe blisters is forced to stop the race.

The threat of those blisters was the elephant in the room for me. What was the point in training if I could not prevent blistering? In seeking a solution, I remembered my first jobs, which involved manual labour, and how the skin of my palms became thick and tough from working outside. I had to find a way to reproduce the same result on my feet.

In my talks, I present a short video of me moving my feet vigorously in a pile of gravel. In the video, I rub my feet on the rocks in every direction to reach every inch of skin on the top, bottom, and sides. Mixed with coarse sand, the stones themselves are about a centimetre or two across. The video is powerful. The process is clearly uncomfortable, and the audience winces every time.

I then ask them: what would happen if I rubbed my feet in gravel for five hours the day before the race? The answer? Nothing good. In fact, I would injure my feet. And what if I rubbed them for ten minutes once per week? I would not injure myself, but my skin would not become tougher, either. But if I rubbed them in the stones for just one or two minutes, every single day for the two months preceding the race, the result would be incredible. The skin of my feet would toughen up without becoming injured. Of 134 runners, I was the only one to finish the race without any blisters. Not a single one!

One step at a time. If this book contained only five words, that is what I would have written: one step at a time! It's an expression that summarizes my whole journey and all my achievements. It's amazing what we can do when we do just a little every day.

Barely 100 runners finished the race; many had to abandon the challenge because of foot injuries. I remember my first day on the gravel beach, in the middle of autumn, rubbing my feet in the stones to the bewildered stares of passersby. Even I wondered if I was losing my mind!

As though the desert wanted to confirm or reinforce what I had learned, the dunes themselves taught me an extraordinary lesson. I didn't know it at the time, but dunes move and change. Ranging from the size of a building to the size of a small mountain, they are beautiful and powerful. Despite their size, they move. In one spot one day, a dune can be 500 metres to the left or to the right the next week. It's the wind that moves them, one grain of sand at a time.

The wind can blow up to 200 kilometres per hour, but if it blows for only a minute, the dune won't move. However, the wind does not need to blow very hard to move a mountain of sand, as long as it blows consistently.

Dunes show us that the size and significance of our actions are irrelevant. What matters is the frequency, the value, and the intention behind each action. All goals, big or small, are achieved one step at a time. It is as simple as that. In anything we do, we start with a first step, and then, like the wind pushes the dunes, we take one step at a time.

It was through this lesson, so simple yet so profound, that I was able to run across Canada a few years later. The task was Herculean, but I achieved it easily, by taking it one step at a time.

It's amazing what we can do when
we do just a little every day.

Climbing and Descending

Mount Everest has a base camp, followed by four other camps at higher altitudes. Once arrived at Base Camp, we stay for about a week. Rest, equipment preparation, climb planning, and team meetings fill our days. This week also plays an important role in acclimatizing our bodies to the altitude. Upon arrival, our steps are slow and painful, breathing is hard, and the slightest effort becomes a test of endurance. But slowly, the body adapts by producing more red blood cells to carry oxygen more efficiently. Patience, humility, and respect for the altitude are important, since everyone adapts at a different pace.

A week later, the big day arrives. The climb and the dream of a lifetime are suddenly underway. Base Camp (5,300 metres) and Camp 1 (6,100 metres) are separated by a dozen hours of effort. Once at Camp 1, we are again forced to stay put for a few days to continue the acclimatization process. Camp 1 is nothing more than a small open space on the mountain-side. Unlike Base Camp, where there are a few amenities for comfort, Camp 1 is completely deserted, and the days spent there can be quite monotonous. The next step always surprises novices, because after a few days at Camp 1, we descend back to Base Camp.

Everest is not scaled all at once. Climbers must ascend and descend several times to help the body gradually adjust to the altitude and prepare for the final push to the peak.

Back in Base Camp after our first stay in Camp 1, we spend a few more days inspecting our equipment, resting, and watching the weather. When the time is right, we climb back to Camp 1, spend a few more days there, then climb to Camp 2 at 6,300 metres above sea level. Although it isn't much higher, it's an excellent threshold for more acclimatization. After a few days at Camp 2, it's back down to Base Camp.

Climb and descend, climb and descend. It's a perilous process, with pitfalls, unforeseen problems, obstacles, and stumbling blocks throughout. No matter how much you love the mountain and mountain climbing, this endless return to square one is exhausting, both physically and mentally. It's a demanding, intimidating, and sometimes depressing process. Nevertheless, it's the only way to reach the summit, and the only way the body can adapt to the altitude.

We can learn several lessons from this. First, this process illustrates the vast difference between *what we want to do* and *what we must do* to achieve it. The temptation to abandon the mission arises with doubt or discouragement. Abandonment is often preceded by phrases like *this is not what I expected, this is not how I imagined it.* Unsurprisingly, *what we want to do* is always pleasant and rewarding. Of course I want to participate in a marathon! Of course I want to enjoy financial success! Of course I want a romantic relationship that helps me grow! But *what I have to do* to achieve those things, that part is not always so easy.

Abandonment is often due to a lack of differentiation between what you want and what you must do to achieve that desire. Things aren't going as planned? Are you tempted to give up? Protect your dream by refusing to let the less pleasant parts (what you must do) pollute your goal (what you want to do).

On Everest, we start the same process again a few days later. We leave Base Camp once again, reach Camp 1 ten hours later, and stay for a night of sleep. We reach Camp 2 the next day, and after spending a few days there, we make our first attempt for Camp 3 at 7,200 metres above sea level. This is where things get more difficult, partly because from this point onward, oxygen cylinders are almost essential. The first visit to Camp 3 is very significant. We try to spend a night without our oxygen cylinders, in maximum discomfort, so that our bodies can become acclimatized to the ambient conditions as much as possible.

> The greater the discomfort, the
> greater the transformation.

The first attempts to climb Everest took place in the 1920s. For 30 years, every ascent was made in one shot, with no descent stages, and with no success. After 30 years of trial and error, the summit was finally reached for the first time in 1953. In fact, it was by climbing in multiple stages and including many returns to lower altitudes that Sir Edmund Hillary was able to reach the Everest summit, the first successful climb. Imagine the first time a climber suggested going back down. Imagine how absurd and counterintuitive that idea must have seemed. The road to success is often like this, especially when you tackle the impossible.

Climb and descend, climb and descend. Crossing countless crevices, braving the cold and the altitude. Climb and descend. Repeat. Whether in business or in our personal lives, we are constantly being told that we must get out of our comfort zone. Is there anyone left who can hear this expression as meaningful, when it is so overused that it has become a cliché?

Let's try to restore meaning to this expression. Leaving your comfort zone does not simply mean you should do difficult things, go off the beaten track, or take risks. In fact, you must understand that allowing discomfort can be completely useless and even counterproductive if it is not done well. Like a climber who carefully chooses the next stage on the mountain, you must find and follow the next logical step.

Leaving your comfort zone and moving towards the next logical step is a process of experimentation to produce a specific result. The exercise requires a clear mind and self-awareness. Which skills should I seek to learn? Which aspect of my personality am I trying to improve? Is the lesson given by the experience outside my comfort zone in line with my goals? For leaving your comfort zone to be effective, you must find the logical next step that contributes to your growth.

Before acting, clearly identify the reason you want to leave your comfort zone and set the goal that you intend to achieve.

I'll say it again: I'm awful at sports. The first time I ran, I managed to run about 250 metres, and that was as far as I could go. I was in my twenties, but I was not in shape. I certainly could have signed up for a marathon the next day—God knows that it would have gotten me out of my comfort zone! My family and friends would have applauded my courage, but I would have reaped very little benefit, if any, by doing such a thing. At the time, I was not mentally equipped to persevere long enough to reach the starting line. I was not in the physical shape I needed to be in to survive months of training. Nor did I have the technical knowledge to train properly, and I would probably have injured myself. The next logical step I had to take was to run 500 metres, a few steps further.

How do you identify the next logical step? It should awaken a fear, but failure or the worst possible outcome should not lead to disaster. It should also be realistic enough to achieve in your current circumstances and with your current abilities, provided that you can make more effort than you have in the past. In other words, regardless of the outcome, success or failure, the next logical step is a small step forward that must give rise to a positive learning experience no matter what happens. By directing yourself patiently and humbly towards the next logical step, failures are never disastrous; instead they constitute small adjustments that are normal and essential to our development. Choosing the next logical step means going home with a smile after a failure and welcoming what you just learned, eager to apply the lesson to try a new experience.

Leaving your comfort zone means finding the next logical step.

The act of moving forward and the principle of imbalance, figuratively and literally, are inseparable. By walking or running, we create an imbalance by launching the body forward with every step and each stride. For a split second, we fall into the void. Each instant of imbalance is followed by a muscle reaction to stabilize the body before moving forward again. Moving forward is thus accepting that we will fall. Moving forward is the result of thousands of small adjustments.

Our professional and personal growth must rely on the same principle: small logical imbalances every day, followed by adjustments, to stimulate growth and continue to move forward. Growth does not require a major imbalance or great upheaval. It's the consistency that is crucial.

Alignment

To protect my chances of reaching the summit of Mount Everest, I had to make a very difficult decision two weeks before the final push. While the entire team was preparing to move from Camp 2 to Camp 3 for a night of acclimatization, I fell ill, to the point that I was struggling to acclimatize to the altitude. I made the decision to pack up and descend back to Base Camp. As heartbreaking as it was, it was because of that decision that I was able to reach the Everest summit two weeks later. From this experience I drew the concept of alignment, which is crucial to achieving our goals, both personal and professional.

When I give talks at companies, I often ask the following questions to the audience: *Who in this room is busy at work? Who is completely overwhelmed with their tasks?* The answer, verbal or silent, is always the same. Every hand goes up; everyone chuckles while the room hums with muttered exchanges about the breakneck pace of their work lives. In fact, this pace is standard for many of us. At night, when our partners ask how our day was, we say that it was crazy, that it was ridiculous.

I ask another question: *Who here is efficient?*

The room stills. Laughter is replaced by hesitant glances between audience members. A few hands go up. For the rest of the audience, at best, the consensus is that they don't really know, but they hope that they are efficient.

Efficiency and productivity are important topics to companies because they are crucial for good business. Overused and mentioned at almost every meeting, these words have unfortunately lost some of their significance. Being busy on a task is not the same as being efficient. Efficiency is the alignment of four targets: the final goal, the sub-goals, the decisions and actions taken in view of this goal and sub-goals, and finally, the scale to measure relevance. These four targets are organized in a pyramid, with the final goal at the top. Just like our fastmoving world, the targets are also moving. Because of this, alignment is a challenge that requires agility and flexibility.

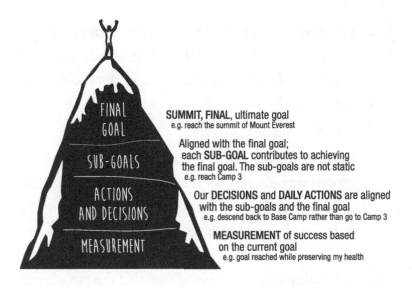

SUMMIT, FINAL, ultimate goal
e.g. reach the summit of Mount Everest

Aligned with the final goal;
each **SUB-GOAL** contributes to achieving
the final goal. The sub-goals are not static
e.g. reach Camp 3

Our **DECISIONS** and **DAILY ACTIONS** are aligned
with the sub-goals and the final goal
e.g. descend back to Base Camp rather than go to Camp 3

MEASUREMENT of success based
on the current goal
e.g. goal reached while preserving my health

When I made the decision to return to Base Camp instead of climbing to Camp 3 with the rest of the team, my sub-goal of reaching Camp 3 changed and was replaced by my need to maintain my health and strengthen my chances of reaching the summit. My actions corresponded to my new sub-goal. If I had continued the climb to Camp 3, that action would have seriously compromised my chances of attaining my final goal. Also, by assessing my opportunities to reach the summit in light of this revised sub-goal, my momentary disappointment in not joining my team became the satisfaction of doing what I needed to reach my final goal.

Let's see how this theory works in everyday life.

There are people who are very successful, but who are never happy. Such people probably only measure the final goal, and if they do not reach it, they will not be happy. And since the final goal never lasts very long, they are never happy for very long! In other words, they measure their success based solely on the final goal, failing to celebrate the small victories that brought them to the top.

Let's look at another example.

In a project, people often become obsessed with the end goal, put the cart before the horse, skip steps, and concentrate on the wrong priorities, to the point that their day-to-day actions do not align with sub-goals. For example, it's pointless to look for a trailer to use to cross Canada before having secured funding and before being sure that the project will actually start. Aligning our actions with our sub-goals helps us become and remain efficient and productive. This alignment also enables many projects to see the light of day rather than die early on in the process. It's important to prepare your project well before seeking financial support. It's important to prepare your proposal and pair it with an alluring value before trying to sell it. It's important to build a strong relationship with your partner before buying a house. This is alignment. As the saying goes, everything happens in its own time.

Sometimes, our actions become automatic and are no longer in harmony with our sub-goals, and are even less in harmony with our ultimate goal. Humans are creatures of habit and comfort. The actions we take by habit may no longer be the ones that will help us take the final steps to our ultimate goal. That's why we must regularly review how relevant our actions are and make sure we are making good use of our energy and our valuable time.

Hope is not a strategy. Do you hope to succeed or do you want to succeed? The difference between the two is enormous. Skeptical? Say it out loud: *I hope to succeed.*

Not very convincing, is it?

Now try this: *I will succeed.*

To reach a goal, you must first set a target. It may seem a little obvious, but if I choose to reflect on this, it's because many people do not pursue goals. For many, life and work become mechanical actions. Eat, work, sleep, and repeat the next day. They are not necessarily unhappy, but strictly speaking, they have no clear destination.

To reach a goal, you must first set a target.

Whether it's a promotion, a work target, breaking your record in a marathon, or a sabbatical to travel around the world, you need a plan to achieve a goal. Set up your pyramid with your goal at the top, and list the sub-goals and appropriate actions that will carry you to it. I promise you will enjoy a lot of success. It is simple and effective.

Hearing Silence

Sahara Race, Day 4

My daily ranking was improving day by day, and the race was going well, even though the difficulty of the competition had exceeded all my expectations. My performance goals were forgotten on the first day, so the adventure had taken on a very different meaning. We were running against ourselves. We were running to discover what we were made of. Lost in this incredibly homogeneous environment, the real exploration became internal. Nature had done its work, and had done it quickly and magnificently. Nature trampled us in the first hour, picking us up like seeds on the wind to take us to a path it felt was much more important.

This new quest made evening conversations extremely interesting. Our only concern was that the experience should be positive. Nobody talked about rankings; instead, we discussed what the finish line would mean. We talked about our past experiences, about what had led us to sign up for the race. Everyone had their own story. Willem Pennings, a Californian in his 40s, admitted to me that he had had serious substance abuse problems in the past, and that running had saved his life. A Korean man, who was far from being in great physical shape, had signed up to the race to prove to his fiancée that he was willing to do anything for her. He had promised to ask her to marry him once he finished the race.

With all of us in the same boat, forced to face ourselves, our fears, and our limitations, camaraderie grew. No matter what position we were in when we crossed the daily finish line, in fourth place or in 42nd place, we celebrated the accomplishment of each person. Our position was the best we could do that day, it was always the best of ourselves. First or last, the internal journey was the most demanding part of the adventure, and we were all fascinated by both.

My best memory of the Sahara Race was when I heard real silence for the first time in my life. Imagine running in the sand and the endless dunes. There was no vegetation, and no other participants for miles around. No cracking branches, no soothing sounds, no birdsong, not even wind rustling grass and leaves. Nothing. Nothing but the void, absolute silence. It's a powerful experience that forces you to reflect inward.

We spend a lot of time looking for answers and finding our way. We seek to achieve goals that define us. We want success and, reasonable or not, the approval of others. We spend time and resources and often a lot of energy. Phew! It's all very exhausting. But what if all these answers already exist within us? What if it's not about finding answers, but about listening to them?

I'm not saying that you have to travel all the way to the Sahara to discover yourself. This silence can also be achieved at home. What I mean is figurative silence and, in fact, figurative noise—the noise that distracts us and pulls us away from what we really want to do. This includes expectations from others, peer pressure, and our desire for approval. To hear and see what is within, you must get rid of this ambient noise.

If I received a dollar every time someone asked me for tips for perseverance, I would be a very rich man. But are they asking the right question? Perseverance is not just the art of learning how to get back up. Perseverance means having a reason to *want* to get through the bad days.

The reason we pursue a dream is often the best indicator to predict its success. Whatever the dream or goal, it's our reasons why we want it that are fundamental. It's the *why* that should be the main source of our motivation, not the goal. My why was to inspire young people with type 1 diabetes, to encourage them to live full lives, wonderful lives, and to help them reach their full potential, despite their condition.

What is your why? That's the biggest question that you have to answer. The why transcends the objective. Why do you want to compete in the Olympics? Why do you want to be a millionaire? When the why of something we do is greater than the obstacle, that obstacle can be overcome. It's simple math.

Why > Obstacle = Success

I suggested earlier that failure is the fuel of success. Our why is the fuel for perseverance. How do you find your why? Often, it's through silence and the void.

We don't look for our why, we listen to it.

It is not about looking for answers, but listening to what's within us. The answers—and your why—are there. Listening is not necessarily easier than seeking, since it requires a lot of courage. You need to have the courage to accept the answers you will hear.

Wherever we look, others try to make us believe that we need more to succeed and be happy, whether it's the clothing size of models in magazines, our neighbour's shiny new car, or images of rich and perfect people in ads. Worse, our peers, who take pictures of their lives and post them to social media, show only the best moments, using the perfect filter and angle to isolate and embellish an image that is not a true reflection of reality. Working in the shadows, false gods often set false goals for us. At first glance, our goals seem to be our own: become rich, run in a marathon, become a doctor, buy a house, start a family.

By creating a state of silence and drawing back from the ambient noise, we can listen to what is really within ourselves. We can then call many of our goals into question.

Are you really passionate about your work or are you looking to achieve social status? Did you marry in your mid-thirties because you really wanted to or because you were following the pack? What is the real reason you want so much material wealth? Did you start to run out of personal interest or because all your friends were? Are you investing in a house because that's apparently what people do when they grow up, but to the detriment of the company you dream of launching?

Are the goals you've set really yours, or are they the result of the noise buzzing in your environment? What would you do if no one would judge you? What would you do if the financial aspect disappeared completely from your life? What would be your dream or your job? What kind of company would you launch if you were guaranteed to succeed? The answer is not in the Sahara or at the other end of the world. It is quite close, within you, and all you need to do is slow down, pay attention, and listen.

Do we need to start listening, or stop ignoring? The worst thing is that the crazy idea we hold dear, the one we would like to do more than anything else in the world—we already know what it is. It's not even about listening anymore, we simply have to stop ignoring it! That crazy idea often frightens us, so we stifle it, ignore it, and set it aside, waiting for the opportune moment. It can be terrifying to listen to who we really are, hear the call, our mission. For example, someone who comes from a family of academics can find it hard to answer the call they feel towards an entrepreneurial or musical career. I come from a family where education was very important. We never talked about art and culture at home. It took me 15 years to realize that I was much more of an artist than someone dedicated to academics. Today, I write and earn a living by giving talks. I rebuffed this desire and the calling for far too long. Still, it was me. My goals were not really mine, even though I was convinced otherwise.

Goals that are not our own can still be attractive. However, it is important to note that we are drawn in only by the final result: having a lot of money, being a celebrity, enjoying the status of certain professions, being in top physical shape, and so on. If the only reason you want to practise a profession is the social status it will give you, but you hate the classes you have to take to earn the diploma, what makes you think you'll enjoy the work once you've graduated? If you hate running, but you're signing up for a marathon because everyone else seems to be a runner these days, what makes you think that you'll be proud of having participated in the marathon?

> If you don't enjoy the process, what makes
> you think you'll enjoy the result?

When our motivations are external to us, we chase goals that are not our own. Even if you are doing it to please your mother whom you love, if that's the only reason motivating you towards a goal, then you're on the wrong path. In a world where we can be anything we want to be, why not be ourselves? Silence helps you find your why, your motivation for doing things for yourself and, consequently, helps you find happiness in the process. By finding happiness in the process rather than in the result, we stop looking for happiness, stop chasing after it, and stop waiting for it to arrive. Instead, we experience it every day.

Listening is often cited as one of the best qualities a person can have. It's a complex task because it requires us to temporarily set aside our opinions, knowledge, beliefs, and perceptions.

I don't mean that you should throw out your principles. Listening is difficult because it requires us to silence ourselves not just in the usual way, but also internally. We have to prevent our perceptions from interfering with the information we are receiving.

False listening means being silent without trying to understand the other person, and instead waiting for our turn to bombard them with our opinions. We frequently ask questions for which we expect specific answers.

Linguistics calls this type of exchange a phatic expression, which isn't used to communicate a message, but instead serves to maintain contact between the speaker and the listener.

For example, when you arrive at work in the morning, a colleague asks, "Hi, how's it going?" as they pass you in the hallway, waiting for a positive response, a short, "Good, thanks! And you?"

> In choosing to listen, you accept that
> you don't choose the answers.

Before asking a question, you must ask yourself whether you have the courage to accept the answer. Naturally, this is true not only for interactions with others, but also for interactions with yourself when you decide to cut out the ambient noise to listen to the answers within.

Sometimes these answers can be surprising and shocking. Will you have the courage to listen and accept them?

Pain Relief

Pain was a constant companion over the nine months of my run across Canada. The aches, the stiffness in my smallest movements, and the struggle of moving became my daily reality. Slowly, the body and mind adjust to this new reality. My pain threshold changed and my tolerance to discomfort increased over the months. Even if I suffered greatly, it was what I had chosen to do, and I did not complain about it. I gradually forgot what it was like not to be in pain. In the weeks and months that followed after the journey, I rediscovered what it was like to live without pain. I was sometimes even amazed, especially in the first weeks, at how different life was without all the pain.

I frequently look at the archives, at the photos and videos of this great adventure. What impresses me the most is the weather I ran in during the first months. Storms, extreme cold, and snow-covered roads were my lot in life. For two months, I put on as many layers as I needed to brave the cold and run 40 kilometres in -10, -15, and sometimes even -30 degree weather. Looking at these images, I can't always understand how I found the energy I needed to do it. I'm often the first to wonder how I was able to achieve this goal. Still, during the crossing itself, I never had the impression that the situation was that difficult. When I recall my other memories, like in the mountains, in triathlons and in the Sahara, I now see many of those situations as insane, unthinkable, and even atrocious.

When our reality changes, our body and mind adapt. Over time, I've come to realize that when we are experiencing a situation, we don't realize how well or how poorly things are going. Fear often disappears once we're knee-deep in the situation. Stress always precedes the anticipated event, but fear almost always fades once we have crossed the starting line. Recall your first marathon or your first competition. Stress mixed with excitement during the weeks preceding the race. The day of the event, joy and terror combined into a bubbling mix of emotions that caused that famous sensation of butterflies in your stomach, some colourful, others black with fear. But as soon as you crossed the starting line, those feelings evaporated. As soon as you became immersed in a new reality, a new context, it became your new normal. During the hours of the challenge, you experienced ups and downs, good minutes and bad, maybe even good hours and bad, but your anxiety almost completely faded away.

> Once we become immersed in a new reality,
> in a new context, it becomes our new normal.

Why is this important to remember? Because it's this principle that enables us to move forward in every circumstance. If you know that a new reality quickly becomes a new normal, you can take that scary first step with much more confidence.

I have been stressing the importance of the first step since the page one of this book. Up to now, I have talked about the first step as a literal step, and I've defined it as an action. That first step is often the first step of a process of transformation that causes great upheavals in our lives. These critical moments of change happen several times over the course of a life, such as at the end of an important relationship, during a change of career, or during a big move.

However, there is no single first step. The first step as an action is in fact the first of many first steps. Each transformation, each effort has its own first step. That's why we have to broaden our concept of what a first step is, from an action to an attitude. Like physical or mental endurance, the art of the first step is a skill that we gradually acquire, a talent that we hone through training and practice. It's not an ability we have or lack; it's not an inherited trait. Learning to be bold enough to take the first step is like learning to play guitar: with doing a lot of practice.

> The art of the first step is much more
> of a philosophy than an action. It is
> a mindset. It's a way of moving forward,
> exploring, growing, and learning.

In the end, I took millions of steps to run across Canada. Except for the first hundred, they all hurt. People often ask me how much anti-inflammatory or pain relief medication I had to take.

The answer is none. In nine months, I did not take a single pill, and I did not take even the mildest pain reliever.

First of all, these drugs significantly hinder the process of recovery and muscle repair. Many studies have shown that pain relievers neutralize a lot of training. In my case, rapid recovery was the technique that allowed me to keep going. After each marathon, I had to do everything I could to recover for the next day.

My recovery strategy was carefully designed and required almost as much effort as the marathon itself. Immediately after the run, I ingested a lot of protein and carbohydrates to promote muscle recovery. It required military discipline, since the cells are particularly open and capable of recovery in the 30 minutes following physical exercise. At the end of each day, I filled a bath with cold water and ice, which I sat in for 12 long minutes. I had a love-hate relationship with the ice bath. It's a miraculous treatment for reducing inflammation, preventing injuries, and speeding up recovery, but it was also torture. Following the bath, I spent 30 minutes in recovery boots. These canvas boots cover the entire leg and exert compressor-regulated pressure to activate circulation. This eliminates toxins and speeds up recovery. I then attached a device to my calves. The size of a wrist watch, the device sends electric signals that stimulate the common peroneal nerve of the knee, increasing blood circulation and once again speeding up recovery. I also had to get enough good sleep, eat healthy (and not too much alcohol), and resist temptations that would affect my physical fitness. In other words, it was thanks to everything I did when I wasn't running that I was able to succeed when I did run.

> It's the invisible part of our efforts that
> makes the visible part of success possible.

As we'll see in the last chapter, success is a point in time. It's what we do in the shadows that lets us shine: training at five a.m. before going to work, spending hours developing a business plan, planning a trip for months before leaving, saving a few dollars over years to eventually buy a rental property, the products we develop before finding commercial success, and so on.

The other reason I chose not to take anti-inflammatories was the pain itself. To run 7,200 kilometres in nine months, I could not afford to mask the pain, because the information pain provides is vital to an athlete's success.

For athletes, pain is a source of valuable information. When I feel pain in my knee, the time when it appears—before, during, or after a run—signals a completely different injury. Is the pain limited to a specific part of the body? Is it spreading? Is it getting worse or easing up? Pain provides critical information about the type of injury and therefore about what treatment is appropriate. The intensity and evolution of pain, as well as when it appears, are determining factors that an athlete uses to react appropriately. But if athletes mask their pain with drugs, it becomes impossible to know if they have to slow down, speed up, continue, or stop. It is also impossible for them to know whether the treatments they are using are appropriate and whether the injury is healing or worsening.

For example, consider knee pain that appears 25 minutes into a race. If, with rest, your knee can tolerate 45 minutes of running a week later, then the injury is healing well. But in order to measure and monitor how an injury is developing, you cannot mask the pain. Ironically, the pain we fear is actually one of an athlete's most valuable tools.

Is this only for athletes? We must not put a salve on our careers, our workplaces, or our whole company and its culture. This also applies to our personal lives. In business, we must create a climate where information, painful or otherwise, can circulate freely without being masked. Obviously, failures, mistakes, projects and processes that do not work, slip-ups, entrepreneurial setbacks, and corporate defeats always hurt. These are the wounds of a company. Too frequently, often in the name of the political contest that freezes many companies, these injuries are ignored or hidden. We choose to look elsewhere, where things are rosy. By avoiding feeling pain, opportunities are lost.

I was young and inexperienced when I got a job as a pharmaceutical representative for one of the world's largest drug and medical device manufacturers. A few months later, my boss informed me that she would spend a day on the road with me. Terrified, I slept poorly the whole week before her ride-along. To ensure I would make a good impression, I carefully prepared an itinerary that would just so happen to focus on my best clients. I even took care to notify some of them that "a head office visitor" would be coming with me to our next meeting. My car was perfectly clean and the day went smoothly. All my clients greeted us with open arms and had nothing but good things to say about our company. In my opinion, I had made sure the day had gone off without a hitch.

In fact, what I had done was apply a large dose of anti-inflammatory drugs. No useful information resulted from the experience. I did not learn anything, and I did not allow my boss to contribute to my professional development. Worse, we were unable to measure the real situation in my territory, and we did not obtain any information that could have helped us improve our service and our products.

It's by confronting resistance, by facing our worst clients, and by not masking information that a company can really grow. In fact, if I had introduced my worst clients to my superior, I would have shown honesty and transparency. I was 25 years old and I had a lot to learn. Camouflaging my inexperience behind a trick was definitely not the way to grow. I hadn't yet grasped the power of discomfort and resistance.

That day, I chose instead to put up a wall that would prevent any growth.

Discomfort and resistance are essential ingredients to self-transcendence.

Facing resistance is the most effective way of learning and growing personally and professionally. When we don't try to use a salve on our careers or personal relationships, we demonstrate a great virtue: humility. I highly recommend Kevin Briggs's TED talk, "The bridge between suicide and life". During his 30 years of service, Sergeant Briggs of the San Francisco police responded to hundreds of distress calls made by people preparing to jump to their death from the Golden Gate Bridge. Under his watch, only two of those people ultimately jumped. Briggs explains his success by saying that whatever the extent of his knowledge, training, and expertise, he always listens to each person and tries to understand them. Briggs teaches us to listen to understand. Not to judge, argue, or criticize. Listen to understand.

Do not apply a salve to your professional or personal life; this means listening to your colleague, client, or partner to understand their complaints, needs, and reality and to understand what would change their world and what would transform their business. Not to be right, but to understand their position, their concerns, and their path. Listening to understand is trying to see a situation or problem from the other person's point of view. It's stepping back from our own perception of what's good or bad, logical or not, appropriate or not, to examine the context from another person's perspective, based on their views and emotional baggage, to understand all the experiences that have shaped their opinions, beliefs, and temperament.

Choosing not to apply a salve to your life is choosing to meet resistance head-on and choosing an uncomfortable truth over comforting lies. It's choosing to sincerely consider what needs changing and improving. And therefore, it's necessarily choosing to face failure more often.

Fear of failure often stops us from beginning, from throwing ourselves into a project, from trying. This fear takes different forms: performance anxiety, fear of leaving your job to start your own company, fear of the unknown, fear of making a mistake by ending a relationship, fear of being inadequate, fear of applying to a new job, fear of making a bad choice by accepting a job offer, fear of leaving everything behind to chase an opportunity halfway around the world.

At talks, people often ask me to discuss failure and more specifically, how to overcome it. We are afraid of what hurts us, what prevents us from succeeding, and disappointment. When fear of failure appears, we feel stressed and anxious, to the point that we sometimes implement temporary solutions to block out the anxiety, like an upbeat song to restore our spirit or a series of positive affirmations. These tricks can help us overcome fear for a short time, but in reality, they're only a temporary distraction, and fear of failure is still very present.

As soon as we try to overcome failure, we put ourselves on the wrong path. Trying to overcome failure is just treating the symptom instead of the cause. That's why we shouldn't look to overcome or defeat failure. Instead, we have to change our perception of failure and look at it in a positive light so that it no longer scares us. Failures are only failures if we abandon our goals! The real magic is that as long as we get back up to continue, failure changes its name and becomes a learning opportunity.

I suggest discussing points of resistance rather than failure. It's a much more positive concept, and it's much more consistent with the positive resulting from failure. Instead of the end of the road, resistance is a detour or a slowdown. In a car, we are able to notice many more details about the landscape when we drive slowly. To improve the technique of athletes they train, coaches film them then slow the playback down to study their actions. Since points of resistance put on the brakes and slow us down, they give us an opportunity to improve our awareness and understanding of the relationship between our thoughts, our emotions, and our actions, and to become aware of the adjustments we have to make to our lives.

Once our perception of failure has been transformed to something positive and valuable, we stop being afraid of it. Once we stop being afraid of failing, we become more eager to learn. Since it is indispensable, failure becomes an ingredient.

No longer the missing recipe or the burned cake, failure is the essential ingredient to a successful cake. Now we have a tool that we actively use to produce results.

Failure is an ingredient, not an end.

In sports, business, and personal lives, failure should not be overcome, it should be used. In any event, failure is inevitable. It's universal: every person experiences it many times in their life. We tend to forget and sometimes believe that we are the only ones in the world to experience bad times. The problem with failure is also that when it occurs, we see ourselves *as* that failure and believe ourselves to be incapable or inadequate. We are not failures, we are just experiencing failure. The fear of being inadequate is the root of our fear of failure.

You are not your failures.
You are experiencing failure.

Consider yourself an observer, a bit like you're looking at a painting in a museum. This painting is beautiful, I don't like that one. The beauty you see does not determine what you are. Of course, this does not mean separating ourselves from our responsibilities or from the role we played in the failure. It's possible that a specific failure is the result of negligence, a lack of dedication, or oversight on our part, or even the result of our incompetence. Even so, look at failure as you would a painting, by analyzing it and looking for solutions to improve the situation. How can I become more competent? What readings, training, and experiences could help? How can I develop my discipline and my consistency in training? If you persist and try again, failure will be a positive point of resistance, an opportunity for learning, a valuable lesson that you can use to win and reach your goal.

We don't have to fear or try to overcome failure. Instead, we should welcome it, cherish it, use it, and even seek it out to move forward. It is an essential ingredient to our growth.

A year before I began my run across Canada, a dozen executives working for potential sponsors asked me the following question: Is this possible? Armed with my PowerPoint, I presented my project. At every door I knocked on, I was asked the same question. Even when a sponsorship was authorized, the elephant was always in the room: is running 170 marathons in nine months without injury even possible? For most people, asking the question was answering it.

From my perspective, I had been working on this project for a year and the question had never even entered my mind. I had never asked myself if it was possible. I never wondered about the risk of injury. I simply took for granted from day one that it was possible. I ordered my brain to run 7,200 kilometres. At the time, I had no idea of what kind of power I had just exercised: giving orders to my brain.

Many books discuss the law of attraction. Personally, I do not believe that reciting a list of your goals and desires every morning based on this supposed law is a valid strategy. I do concede that this theory has merit in helping us stay focused on what we want, but nevertheless hope is not a strategy.

I still believe that nearly unlimited potential exists within each of us. As I said before, my first race was about 250 metres. Ask and you will receive. This adage applies to yourself and to your own brain, but especially to the latter.

Suppose that you decide to spend a sunny Saturday trying to run the longest distance of your life. Let's say that distance is 20 kilometres. You put on your jogging outfit, tie your running shoes, select your running playlist, and head out. The first kilometres go very well. After 15 kilometres, you're exhausted. At 18, you struggle just to keep going, it's hot out, and you wonder why you had such an absurd idea, but you keep going. Finally, you reach the 20th kilometre, completely drained, and you practically collapse, telling yourself that you could not take another step. You head home, proud of your new record.

Two weeks later, filled with confidence, you decide to try to beat this record. This time, your finish line is at 25 kilometres.

Let's step back for a second. I've done my homework on the exercise side of things. I became interested in sports, I read about sports nutrition, recovery, training for a race, and bodybuilding. I attended many talks on the topic and listened to dozens of experts deliver the results of their studies. I don't know everything, but if there is one thing I know, it's that the body does not change much in two weeks. The body and the skills you used to run 20 kilometres of pain and misery are the same you are planning to use to go 25 kilometres today.

Let's get back to our scenario. So, two weeks later, on another sunny Saturday, you start to run. This time, you breeze past the 15 kilometre mark without much concern. At 20 kilometres, fatigue and pain start to take hold. You slow down considerably, concerned you won't reach your target. At 23 kilometres, you're exhausted. Each step requires immense effort, and you're suffering like you never have before. Finally, after a final kilometre that feels like ten, victory. And what do you say as you reach the 25th kilometre? *I could not take another step.*

Not a runner? You arrive at work, say for a 12-hour shift. Unmotivated, your head in the clouds, you have no desire to be there. The next 12 hours promise to go on forever. You start, and, surprise, the day passes by in the blink of an eye. The following week, it's just the opposite. You go to work for a three-hour shift, and the day takes forever to end.

Researchers have spent years studying the phenomenon I have just described. The concept of anticipatory regulation is at the heart of their discoveries. A study published in the *British Journal of Sports Medicine* (http://bjsm.bmj.com/content/43/6/392) shows that as soon as an order is given to the brain, it makes an inventory of available resources, both physical and mental, then divides them evenly between the starting point and the goal to ensure it does not crash on the way. This is a protection mechanism: always in the aim of protection and safety, the brain re-evaluates needs and makes adjustments, increasing or reducing the rate at which resources are used up. This principle provides a scientific explanation for why, even when completely exhausted, a runner who has just run dozens of kilometres can still sprint when the finish line is in sight. The brain calculates that based on your remaining energy, you can increase your pace and even sprint, since the remaining distance is very short and the end is in sight.

Why should we rejoice in reading this paper? It's because it shows us that we are programmed to succeed. Knowing this, why not set the bar a little higher when we set goals? Why not set bigger goals and dream bigger dreams, knowing that we are programmed to reach the finish line? In my opinion, the expression "ask and you shall receive" is not quite accurate. We should instead say, "order and you will accomplish".

We owe thanks not to this study, but to our survival instinct. The study discusses how the brain allocates resources for protection and safety reasons. When we decide to run 25 kilometres instead of 20, our brain decides to simply run more slowly to ensure the body has enough energy to reach that goal.

The problem with our developed, sophisticated, and technologically advanced society is that our survival instinct is no longer called upon enough. Food is not hard to find, no one is cold at night. I am well aware that not everyone has this opportunity, but the fact remains that satisfying our basic needs is relatively easy nowadays, and we go through life without worrying too much about it.

We are programmed to succeed, of course, but our concept of success is very recent. In fact, for the past two billion years, success has meant surviving. On the evolutionary scale, the technologies we use every day have been around for the equivalent of just a few seconds. Ultimately, we are animals, and we are still programmed to flee the lion to survive.

It's when we use our survival instinct that we do the extraordinary. And since the world we live in no longer activates it, we must do it ourselves. We must choose the right obstacle, risk, or adversity that will enable us to access the potential within ourselves. The lions of the present are challenges and tests we decide to do. What is your lion, the adversity you have consented to?

Consented adversity is the fast track to success and helps us use our full potential. I say use, not create. This potential already exists within us, ready to be used. Some people will spend their lives without accessing their potential, like an impoverished person who lives in misery without ever realizing that millions of dollars are hidden in a box under their bed. And I say it gets you on the fast track, not the easy one. Voluntarily choosing resistance and complexity is also choosing discomfort. Discomfort creates growth, yes, but it's still uncomfortable.

Over the years, by choosing discomfort, I've learned to appreciate and even prefer it. People often ask if I'm content in difficult situations, if I enjoy being in pain, or even if I'm masochistic. It's a reasonable question. Being in pain doesn't make me happy, but learning and growing do.

Almost everyone finds something extraordinary, impressive, and inspiring, whether it's Everest or something else. We admire people who achieve the impossible, because what they do is incredibly difficult. Setting a goal is not very complicated. It's when things get complicated that we are truly tested. If you think about it, the hard part is what makes the challenge so extraordinary. It's precisely the reason a challenge is so exciting. In the mountains, during my run across Canada, and in the Sahara, I had several moments where everything seemed lost. Each time, I told myself that it was this moment that made the summit or the finish line so valuable to me. It was through those difficulties that the challenge became interesting, and therefore what drew me to these athletic competitions.

The difficult part of a challenge is the part that offers the most opportunity. Today, I sometimes even find myself waiting impatiently for resistance, almost eagerly, as if that adversity were confirming that I was preparing to learn something, to grow, and to discover another part of my own potential.

The greater the adversity, the greater the reward.

Choosing adversity is choosing to increase the size of the reward. This reward comes in many shapes, including self-esteem, pride, the honour of having tried, wisdom gained on the road, a sense of accomplishment, and experience.

Ego

Halfway between Thunder Bay and Winnipeg, the road seemed endless. The weather was not always good, but regardless of how the sky looked, Patrick and I were still out there every day. These long weeks were by far the most difficult part of the campaign. The endless forest, the summer without friends, the cool and gloomy weather; every day seemed the same as the one before, it was crazy. Wake up, drive in the truck to reach the starting point, run through the middle of nowhere, go back to the trailer, eat dinner, and go to bed. I still took some pleasure in running, and the calm was certainly soothing, but the isolation was difficult for me.

The run was quite painful. The route was far from flat, and every day had its own series of challenges, so I could never really predict how the marathon would unfold. Since we did not participate in as many events and since the agenda was a little less packed, sometimes I ran further than planned. On several occasions during the Northern Ontario leg, I did 45-kilometre days. Meanwhile, Patrick kept himself busy in the truck by planning the logistics for upcoming events, taking pictures, or simply enjoying a few minutes of relaxation.

On the PR side of things, it was decidedly a less hectic time, and I think we were recovering from the extremely demanding weeks that we had just been through in the Montreal-Windsor corridor. We stopped to refill our food supplies at every major town in Northern Ontario. The trailer was always fully loaded, and I'd be lying if I said we ever ran out of beer. God knows that it's impossible to say no to a cold beer after a marathon! Our life was simple, and although at the time the loneliness and isolation were weighing me down, today, it's those times that I miss the most. A fire, a best friend, a marathon, and a beer; what more could you want?

Throughout the journey, I wore a t-shirt branded with the words *Run Across Canada* across the back. I had five made and so I always had the words emblazoned on my back. The shirt was definitely popular. Drivers honked their horns for encouragement as they passed, and passersby would come to talk to me and wish me luck. The horns were a common noise throughout the day, and it was often little things like that that helped me carry on.

One day in August, when I was finally coming up on the Manitoba border, the run was unbearable. It was one of those days when it was a battle just to move forward. Nothing was working, I was struggling to control my diabetes, and my legs simply didn't have any energy left.

One thing is certain: I ran across Canada. People have often spoken to me of my "walk" across Canada or my "trek", which drove me nuts. I had no thought but to deliver my message by showing that we can all accomplish great things, despite the obstacles, that it's precisely thanks to those obstacles that we grow and by choosing them that we become better. That's the message I wanted to leave about my passage. However, my own small pleasure, the personal challenge that I had given myself, was to run from one end of Canada to the other, not to walk. Those who run know how you feel the day after a marathon. Imagine if you had to run another the next day, and the day after that, and the one after that, for nine months. I haven't broken a record, but having completed 170 marathons in nine months in a little more than four hours each time, I am proud.

But that day in August, I was far from running. The road was dull, the weather was gloomy, and my motivation was through the floor. The pain and headaches were increasingly intense with every step, and I had absolutely no desire to carry on. My mood had dropped, too. Unable to run, I slowed down and started walking. That was the exact moment that despair became frustration. How dare I walk, when my shirt clearly said run?

I was frustrated and upset, and my ego felt as bruised as my legs. Angry at myself, at the situation, and, in fact, at everything, I pulled off my shirt. I turned it inside out so that neither the sponsor names nor the *Run Across Canada* logo could be seen, and continued walking while grumbling.

Imagine the scene. A few seconds earlier, before my ego barged in, strangers who crossed my path were giving me words of encouragement. I was a star. Once my shirt was inside out, walking miserably in the middle of nowhere down the Trans-Canada Highway, hundreds of kilometres from civilization, I seemed like a total oddball. A few hours later, I realized that the afternoon had been very quiet, and I had not heard even a single horn. It was only then that I understood my mistake and learned a great lesson.

I had let my ego blind me, turn me away from my message. That day, I had prevented the message from shining. Even the runner that I was had disappeared. Nobody saw me, nobody saw the mission, no one could even say why I was there. When we put our ego before the mission, it loses all meaning and becomes futile.

Conversely, when it was visible, my shirt undoubtedly had an effect on motorists. The shirt was something magical. It emitted a certain aura and signalled something. The speed at which I ran was not important. What mattered was the message. My small successes, my satisfaction in running at a certain speed, none of it really mattered. The mission was much more important than its pilot.

In general, people train for months before a marathon. For amateurs, who constitute the vast majority of runners, it's quite common to walk for a few minutes during a marathon. If someone decides to run 170 marathons, I imagine that they will allow themselves a few minutes of walking here and there. Still, I felt like I was failing by walking.

What I also realized that day is that by holding big dreams close, you take out an insurance policy against failure. People did not see my bad days. They didn't see me walk. Instead, for nearly a year, people saw what I was trying to accomplish, and they started to believe in it, just like I did. People were not paying attention to what I was doing; what mattered was the mission. And since the mission was noble, everyone wanted to be a part of it. It was precisely because the mission was so great that I could walk here and there.

In total, I probably walked about 50 kilometres during the rest of my cross-Canada run, almost always with a smile and never again with my shirt inside out.

At a talk I gave in Cornwall, Ontario, in 2015, I had the pleasure of meeting a man who had recently started running. He ran slowly, but he ran every day. His journey was very inspiring. At his heaviest, he weighed nearly 330 pounds. Nearly under 200 pounds when we met, he confessed that he admired athletes greatly and he felt like an imposter when he ran. Still, he was preparing to run his first half marathon.

In my opinion, being an athlete has nothing to do with the speed at which you run or your weight on the scale. Being an athlete is a mindset, a way of thinking and acting. The day he took the first step to lose weight, this man became an athlete, even though he weighed 330 pounds. Being an athlete is getting up in the morning instead of hitting the snooze button to sleep a little longer. It's having a plan that you follow with strict discipline rather than putting it off until tomorrow. It's accepting sole responsibility for failure and taking steps to improve your lot. Being an athlete is learning from failure and using your victories to progress even further.

The shirt also taught me important lessons in leadership. The truck and trailer, clearly identified by the colours of the campaign and the occasional police escort, were always an amazing spectacle. For nearly a year, I ran on the Trans-Canada Highway and service roads while hundreds of thousands of cars drove past me, carrying hundreds of thousands of people to whom I never had the chance to speak. But I hope that seeing me ignited a flame in some of them, that something clicked. I hope that, as they saw the convoy and the words *Run Across Canada*, some said to themselves, "Wow! If that's possible, then maybe my dream is possible too."

To inspire others,
speaking is rarely necessary; it is enough to act.

True leadership often comes from our actions rather than our words. Our actions always speak louder than words. It's better to do something than to announce that we intend to. Leadership is accessible to everyone and it is also everyone's role.

Whatever our role within a business or our living environment, we all have the power to exercise a profound influence on those around us, simply by our actions, no microphone required. At the end of my twenties, I was living with roommates who were rarely active. I never told them that they should be more physically active. They saw me leave to go running every morning and, like magic, they started running a few months later.

I am first and foremost a triathlete, and most mornings I go swimming. A man who is over 70 years old, blind, and deaf goes to the same pool as I do. He's there almost every morning, and frankly it's inspiring.

When my alarm goes off in the winter, in the dark and the cold, I don't always want to get out of bed, but I know that he'll be there. And I get out of bed. We have never spoken, he doesn't even know that I exist, but he was still the reason I got out of bed. His example, leading through action, helped me become more disciplined and more persistent.

All our actions and all our choices carry meaning. At any moment, people around us are watching us and becoming inspired by us. Each time we make the decision to grow rather than to hinder ourselves, our peers notice. Don't drink and drive, work out instead of sitting in front of the TV, eat well, take time for yourself, take care of your health, end a toxic relationship, refuse to accept verbal abuse at work, make a more ethical choice rather than line your pockets with a questionable contract. Every choice, every decision, every action sends a message to the people around us, and everyone has the power to inspire them to become better, sometimes without our knowledge, without ever having said a word.

Patrick St-Martin

I told Patrick St-Martin about my idea to run across Canada for the first time in the fall of 2012, while we were eating poutine in the middle of the night. Without hesitation, Patrick immediately said that he would come with me.

Some of you may have already crossed Canada by car. The adventure is incredible, and the country is absolutely magnificent. Of course, the road is long and can sometimes seem endless, especially in Northern Ontario, which takes two days to cross by car. Now imagine crossing Canada in a car going at 10 kilometres per hour! That was the monumental task that Patrick had to do during the crossing.

Without Patrick, the crossing would not have been what it was. I would go so far as to say that it would not have been possible. I will be forever grateful for the selflessness he showed throughout the campaign. His good humour and sincere interest in others make him an exceptional person, and it's a great honour, a privilege, and a blessing to count Patrick among my best friends. Sharing the road with him for nine months was among the most influential experiences of my life.

Within weeks, Patrick knew practically everything about my condition. In an era where many feel the need to broadcast their lives on social media, Patrick prefers to go to someone and ask questions. He always knows a little more about us than we know about him. He is interested in other people, not to get something out of them, but simply to get to know them better. He is also interested in what interests us, what our passions are. By going straight to the heart, towards what matters most, Patrick has developed an amazing ability to quickly build solid and personal connections with people.

Over the months, thousands of people followed our journey in the media. People love human stories. Ours was simple: two friends invested in a mission, en route to a destination, on a road filled with obstacles. The premise is universally relatable, and for many, our adventure had nothing to do with Canada or diabetes. They were simply watching a live movie on social media and in the news, and the movie had to be interesting.

Any good movie also has a conflict. But not ours. After a few months on the road, everyone was asking us if we ever bickered and how our relationship was holding up. We had fun from start to finish. We laughed, we played pranks. Every day was amazing. I remember only a single small incident, four days from the finish line, which is not out of the ordinary after all that time, especially with the exhaustion and stress of the finish line helping it along. We were changing towns every week, crossing the path of all sorts of people, and our adventure was being covered by the media. I was suffering every day I ran. Patrick also was there every day. I think that except for my parents, no one has ever done so much for me.

Patrick loves life like no one else. Day after day, he managed to find beauty somewhere. A huge music fan, he wanted to know about the local music scene wherever we went. For his birthday, I set up satellite radio for the truck. Throughout the journey, Patrick spoke to people and asked questions about the local attractions, traditions, and customs of each region.

We lived as nomads, never staying in the same town for more than a week. Like an old married couple, we adopted habits, and each of us had our own tasks and responsibilities. Everything worked out naturally, over time, without having to discuss it. For example, I hate cooking and have no skill in the kitchen at all. I am hopeless in a grocery store, and the idea of putting more time into a meal than it takes to eat is total nonsense to me. Patrick loves cooking. Over those nine months, I cooked only once. Before lunchtime, Patrick would go on ahead with the truck and would wait for me a few kilometres away with a meal ready to eat. He went grocery shopping and enjoyed planning meals. I ate like a king for all those months. However, Patrick, like many people, hates washing dishes. I find it relaxing, so I made sure to always do this task. Patrick did not have to wash even a single fork for the duration of the journey.

I think our success was largely due to the fact that we did not give much importance to small details. Or, rather, we accepted each other's quirks and preferences. As long as the foundation and core values of the relationship were solid, the rest didn't matter. Patrick, again, was amazing. I had a few more rituals than he did. I established a few rules, including a maximum of two pairs of shoes on the trailer's entrance mat. It amused Patrick, who broke the rule more often than not, just to tease me.

Patrick is an artist, a free spirit. Hired first and foremost to handle logistics and events, he showed himself to be extremely creative during the journey. His versatility made him a vital partner. He was driving the escort vehicle, nimbly manoeuvring the 10-metre trailer, and taking care of the logistics, and he was also very talented with the camera, the video camera, and our editing software. Patrick's interest in video and photography grew a lot over the campaign. Everywhere we went, he lugged our equipment to fully document the project. Over the nine months of the journey, Patrick took thousands of photos. He read a lot on the topic, always looking for tricks and new techniques to take better pictures. Today, we have an archive of thousands of photos, many of which are simply spectacular.

Patrick spent a lot of time in the truck. I ran in the direction of traffic while he drove slowly behind me on the shoulder, flashing lights on to warn others of my presence. We also put a sign on the back of the truck to warn motorists that a runner was just ahead of them. In the Maritimes, however, like in Quebec and Ontario, police escort was not possible. We were travelling on service roads, and local authorities deemed it too dangerous for a vehicle travelling at low speed. In those provinces, I ran in the opposite direction of traffic while Patrick would wait five kilometres ahead, always with a joke or special attention.

Initially, I was a little disappointed to lose the escort. But we quickly realized that when Patrick was not driving, he could spend much more time working on the logistics of the journey. With all the event planning, links between the public relations firm and the media, photos, liaisons with local authorities, and equipment maintenance, his days were packed.

Patrick also tried to keep fit by running a few times per week. We purchased free weights and resistance bands. We set up a gym outside when we returned to the trailer, especially in the summer. Patrick trained a little more intensely, while I focused on recovery exercises and stretches. Even though we were together almost all the time, we experienced the Canada crossing very differently. We saw and experienced different things, from a different perspective.

Humour was how we stayed alive, survived boredom, and handled isolation. Everything we did was to have fun, we were able to laugh at everything and nothing. We chose to let nothing affect us negatively. Together, we learned a lot about the key principles of teamwork. Initially, we believed that we were very similar and that we would get along well for that reason. Over the months, we realized that we were actually very different. In discovering each other's strengths and relying on them, our roles took shape. A team's strength does not come from equitably sharing tasks among its members. It comes from focusing on diversifying its members and giving everyone the opportunity to contribute their own strengths.

I often talked about "our crossing" in the media. However, Patrick insisted that I talk about "my" crossing instead, so that the message would be clearer and punchier. His humility was incredible and his dedication to the mission, compelling. A team is strong as long as each of its members is focused on the mission rather than on their status within the group.

With his endless positivity, Patrick was the ideal partner for this mission. I really believe he did half the work.

Patrick, from the bottom of my heart, thank you.

Working Overtime

Completing five or six marathons every week for nine months is not what I am proudest of. Yes, this visible part of the adventure is impressive, but Patrick and I also invested countless hours into the mission after each of these so-called marathons. In fact, a second shift of several hours awaited us at our computers: conference calls, accounting, preparations for upcoming media events, media relations, management of our public relations firm, answering partners' questions, and so on, day after day for nine months.

We also devoted the two years preceding the campaign to planning. Patrick and I felt it unnecessary to plan everything to the smallest detail. Patrick planned an itinerary, chose a route, and decided the approximate dates that I would need to follow to arrive in Vancouver nine months later. We developed a plan of action for media events, but we did not plan the year of the campaign in full. Unable to foresee all the problems we might meet, we knew that too much planning could become hours of wasted work. We had to be flexible, arm ourselves with as many tools as possible, and give life to the project while taking advantage of what the road would offer us. Those two years of planning were mostly spent achieving a feat that I consider monumental: securing funding for the project. I was dreaming big and I needed a lot of money to make my vision a reality. I didn't want to run across Canada pushing a wagon containing my tent and food supply. I also did not want to accomplish something extraordinary unless it would serve others. I wanted to give as much as possible, to leave a legacy, to let a powerful message shine. I wanted an escort vehicle, a bus emblazoned with the project colours. I wanted people who would focus on organizing media events, PR specialists who would ensure the message was shared through media. I wanted the best photo and video equipment for Patrick. I wanted a team of a few people with me on the ground. I wanted someone responsible for the schools component, and someone else for the companies component.

I had imagined hosting a few fundraisers. My first estimates were more than a million dollars. At the end of 2012, I started researching major sponsorships that would allow me to make my vision a reality, and I started to put together a team. Patrick was the first to join me, excited by my vision. Another friend told me that I would never find the million dollars I needed and that no one would pay me a single red cent to run such a long course. I told him he would never work for me.

I didn't want 50 small equipment suppliers; I wanted one or two major sponsors. Even if we were to succeed in obtaining much of the equipment we would need for free, we also needed cash funds, if only to provide our meagre wages.

I didn't want an array of logos arranged in a template that would have diluted the visibility of sponsors. And since each partner has its own expectations, I didn't want to have to meet the expectations of 50 different sponsors. With one or two major partners, I would be able to offer greater visibility while also exerting more control over the message I wanted to convey.

I targeted pharmaceutical manufacturers that offered products for people with diabetes and so began the fishing. I already had a decade of experience in researching sponsorships, and I was ready for a bigger catch.

In the fall of 2013, months later, the funding was secured. I had put in a year of full-time work, evenings and weekends, without pay. I learned a lot doing this and I was able to apply the key lessons to my personal and professional lives. In order to sell your dream, it must have meaning and value to others. You must set aside what you want and ask yourself what the project means to others. Potential partners want to know what they'll get out of the project. Will it promote the values of their brand? What will they gain if the dream is accomplished? What are the values of the project and how will they touch the masses? The key is to ask for nothing to begin with, especially not money. Instead, you must create a movement, a mission that people want to be a part of.

Soon, only two companies remained in the hunt for sponsors. Their representatives and I met several times over several months to develop the project. I rarely mentioned money, and I didn't ask for anything. All my efforts were focused on developing an inspiring and innovative project that was in line with the values and objectives of these companies. Together, we decided on a mission and a project that was exciting enough to hook them, and they started thinking about what they would have to do to be a part of the adventure. If the project was to change the world, they should be there. Otherwise, their competition would do it.

The two companies made what is called an "emotional" purchase. They said yes before we even started talking about money. Of course, negotiations followed, but it was nothing but details. They needed this project.

> Selling your dream does not mean asking
> for something, it means giving.

Selling your dream means giving others the opportunity to be a part of something special. We all want to be part of something special. All you have to do is give this opportunity to others, and they will in turn give you all the support you need.

When it came time to find volunteers who would help us out on different aspects of the project, I noticed a common denominator among the people who helped us the most. If we asked them for help on aspects that they were passionate about, their generosity was boundless. Recent studies have clearly shown that in a business, employees who can make use of their greatest strengths in their work are much more loyal and productive, and are also more satisfied in general. Being able to use our greatest strengths is essential to our happiness and our self-worth. It's very important to ensure that we have the opportunity to shine every day in our professional duties. Otherwise, our sense of fulfillment is at risk.

Obtaining funding to run across Canada is a source of great pride for me. I did not get the million dollars I wanted, but by setting the bar high, I still obtained outstanding results. Ultimately, the project was able to rely on a budget of nearly half a million dollars, which was unheard of for a project like this.

The only snag was that everything was formalized at the last minute, which happens often in cases like this. I received the first payments in early December 2013, and our departure was scheduled for February 2014, 60 days later. In a few weeks, we purchased and painted the vehicles and planned the first media events. After each marathon, Patrick and I spent our time planning. We talked about this as a second marathon, a second shift, or overtime. We would return to our hotel room or to the trailer to work on our computers for hours.

I was too busy to make time for reading, which I quite enjoy, and I quickly started to miss it. Then I remembered that I could listen to audio books or podcasts while running. What luck! When in my life would I have another opportunity to "read" four or five hours a day for nine months? Every morning during my run across Canada, I downloaded content to listen to while I ran: news from CBC and the BBC, episodes about arts, culture, science, and technology, interviews, TED talks, and more. I had never felt so cultivated!

Patrick took a great photo of me while I ran through one of the worst storms of the year. The scene is charged with intensity, the camera technique is breathtaking, I'm wearing a mask, and I appear to be combating the elements. However, I remember very clearly that at the time I was listening to *The Economist*, the British economic news magazine, and that I was inwardly calm, attentive, and organized. That said, there is still a limit to how much motivation you can draw from international news, and, in the late afternoon, when my body was worn out, music picked up the slack.

Since a second shift awaited me after each marathon, my daily run was my time to myself, with four, five, or even six hours of calm, relaxation, interesting podcasts, and above all, a very peaceful run through the outdoors. Sometimes, I had little recollection of the day. I entered a trance-like state and let my legs do their job.

It was a highly appreciated moment of solitude, the only time to myself before the whirlwind of activities that followed each marathon. People often wrote me to ask if they could run a few kilometres with me. Some were more ambitious and wanted to do a half marathon or even a full marathon. I answered yes every time; I wanted this project to belong to everyone, for everyone to be able to take part and participate. But, to be honest, I very much preferred running alone. During the day, I needed the isolation in order to be my best self during interviews with the media and public appearances.

I gave a lot each day. Every rest day also started very early in the morning and was packed with logistical work. On two occasions, in Montreal and later in Alberta, my health declined almost to the point of hospitalization. Physical and psychological exhaustion had reached their peak. A few days without running, without meetings, and without emails got me back on my feet. In the film about my journey across Canada, titled *Un par un*, I confess somewhere in the Prairies that I realized the crossing and these marathons would probably leave permanent marks on me. Today, a few years later, I am doing fine. Wear and tear may be felt later, but only time will tell. In the thick of it, I was suffering and anxious, but also determined to accomplish my mission. Despite the possibility of permanent damage, everything had meaning, and everything was worthwhile. Every day was a new opportunity to change someone's life, and that was enough to give me the energy to continue.

The Wall

To meet the pace of my race across Canada, I ran 40 kilometres per day, five or six days per week. Obviously, there is no training that can prepare anyone for such a challenge. Even in peak form, athletes cannot arrive at a starting line and say they are ready to complete 170 marathons in nine months. Even if they are as physically fit as an Olympic athlete, it takes just a few consecutive marathons for the body to suffer greatly. Barely a few days after starting, I was already in survival mode, and that's where I would stay until I arrived in Vancouver, nine months later.

In any event, training in anticipation of such a challenge is critical. In order for training to be of use, it must respond to two very different things: the challenge and the goal.

The challenge was the daily marathon, the recovery, injury management, nutrition, and other factors. It didn't involve training to learn how to run faster. After five years of striving for my best performance, after having completed several triathlons, I was now entering a world where all concepts of top performance were useless. Instead, I had to learn to run properly to keep going for a long time: to run correctly, more symmetrically, following the best model and best technique to prevent, delay, and reduce the severity of injuries. It was also very important to educate myself on nutrition and other elements of the challenge, such as recovery. Over the years, I had put a lot of time into studying these factors, but I gave them even more attention in the months before the campaign. The key would certainly be recovery. How would I be able to recover sufficiently to tackle the next day, over and over for nine months?

The objective is the final aim. It's the target, the destination that dictates decisions made during the challenge. My objective was to arrive in Vancouver nine months later, approximately 7,200 kilometres away, specifically on November 14, World Diabetes Day. We calculated a schedule including one or two rest days per week, one or two weeks off halfway along, and a few extra days in case of emergency. The margin of error was still very slim. Given that most severe injuries take weeks or even months to heal, I had no room for error. The simple fact of having established an arrival date was very bold and very ambitious.

Clearly establish the difference between your goal and the challenge you must overcome to reach it.

The balance between the challenge and the objective is delicate. First and foremost, you must distinguish between the objective and the challenge, and you must have a complete understanding of each. What is the destination and what is the vehicle that will take you there? Next, the two concepts must be juggled, sometimes focusing more on one, but never forgetting the other. For example, in case of injury or weakness, I had to reduce my day's objective (the challenge) to ensure that I would not break the metaphorical elastic band, thereby protecting the larger objective. Conversely, in situations of laziness and discouragement, it was important to persevere and to maintain my daily mileage to reach the objective in time.

I had good days and not-so-good days, days when I started to run and doubted I could keep going because the pain was so intense, days where the 40 kilometres were perfectly pleasant. The most difficult kilometre was usually not the last, but the 38th. At that stage, the body and mind are bordering on exhaustion, and the brain is very good at finding valid excuses to stop. Mine tried to rationalize stopping, justifying it in the name of the objective, by any means, even begging. The mental battle was arduous, and a few kilometres before the end, the list of excuses or reasons to stop started to grow in my mind: *I'm feeling a little weak, if I keep going to the 40-kilometre mark, I might hurt myself and compromise the entire project. I had a good week, I could do two kilometres fewer and catch up next week. There were a lot of hills today, so even if I stop at 38 kilometres, it will be like I had run 40.*

At 38 kilometres, the brain is doing everything it can to stop. Normal? Totally. Mundane? Not at all. This time of day was extremely crucial. The success of my journey depended entirely on how I reacted to that kilometre. It was a battle every day. To continue, to go those last few kilometres, to resist the temptation to stop, to reach the day's target. We all have this feeling, regardless of our goal. The point is to not create a precedent. The day I let myself stop at 38 kilometres instead of 40 would have opened a door, which would have sealed my fate by creating a precedent that would have become worse with every passing week. The next day or the following week, it would have been much easier for me to stop after 37 kilometres, and the following week, 36. I would have started my daily runs later. I would have lost the consistency that was so important to this project. I had to resist temptation in order to protect my progress and the principle, to avoid creating a precedent, and, above all, to carry on for all the days to come.

What is your 38th kilometre? When does it happen? What precedent might you create and what is the potential cost? Knowing that the temptation to stop is normal, we can implement solutions to resist it, plan for additional resources that will help us continue, and prepare ourselves for this eventuality.

It's important to understand that abandonment is a process, just like success. We rarely abandon a project or dream without warning. Everything begins with doubt and then questioning. We hesitate, and our energy and motivation are quietly drained. Day by day, less time is devoted to the project, the dream. We excuse ourselves by rationalizing the loss of momentum, by finding "good" reasons for putting it off.

Just like success, abandonment is a process.
Since it is governed by the same rules, it can
be sped up, slowed down, or avoided.

Perseverance is much easier than you think. By resisting the temptation to stop at your 38th kilometre, you will avoid becoming ensnared in the negative spiral that leads to abandonment. At talks, I am often asked for tips and tricks for perseverance. The concept of the 38th kilometre is a fundamental aspect. The good news is that perseverance does not require ironclad morale at all times. Just understand that perseverance is a tool and that you must recognize the right time to use it.

Perseverance is a decision, one that you take with you to your 38th kilometre. Perseverance is often a point in time, a crossroads, a choice to stop or continue. Once a decision is made, once the tool has served you, you put it away. The road continues, with its failings, its obstacles, and its points of resistance.

Perseverance is a decision, a point in time.

Persevering does not mean to live as a martyr for days on end, to accept failure, to go backwards, or to work 18 hours per day. Being at your post day after day, rain or shine, that's discipline, not perseverance. Using obstacles as springboards to move forward instead of being discouraged, that's a positive attitude, not perseverance. Discipline, dedication, perseverance, attitude, and consistency are all valuable tools that should be used wisely, in the right way, and at the right time.

Once we had passed through Sault Ste. Marie in Ontario, I had run almost 4,000 kilometres. Patrick was making more and more projections to ensure that I was maintaining a pace that would get me to Vancouver on November 14, World Diabetes Day. Basically, I followed the schedule, but many events in the preceding months had slowed my progress somewhat, to the point that I no longer had a cushion. The smallest injury or unexpected issue would risk compromising my arrival on the 14th. Patrick helped me understand that I would do well to increase my daily mileage and take fewer rest days.

However, at this point of the journey, I hit what runners call the wall. In a marathon, the infamous wall always appears at the three quarters mark of a race. On one side, the distance already travelled is enough for the body and mind to be completely battered and bruised. On the other, the finish line is still too far away to generate an explosion of adrenaline and find the motivation to give whatever you have left. The wall is a moment of darkness in the middle of the race where neither the body nor the mind can overcome it.

What I was experiencing was definitely the wall, but at a much larger scale. I had already travelled 4,000 kilometres and, believe me, everything ached, my muscles and my morale both. The finish line was still 3,200 kilometres away, and now I had to find the energy to add even more kilometres to my daily marathons, and even skip some rest days. To provide a safety cushion to our schedule, I added a few kilometres at the end of each day. The lesson, simple but incredibly important to this story, is that if Patrick and I had made this decision later in the campaign, say, in British Columbia, we never would have been able to catch up. By making it earlier, the added effort was minimal.

The earlier you begin to take small additional steps towards your goal, the easier those steps will be.

If someone had explained all this to me when I was a student, I probably would have avoided a few sleepless nights of studying the night before exams. Similarly, by starting to save when we're young instead of later, in our forties, we save much more and much more easily. This rule applies equally to work in order to achieve our projects and our dreams.

Finding Your Rhythm

One hundred and seventy marathons in nine months without a single injury, not even the smallest blister: is that even possible?

For the first few months after the campaign, I hesitated to speak openly about my lack of injury. I was worried that I would be declared an impostor and that people would doubt I had actually run 40 kilometres every day for nine months. But it's true that I never suffered any injury during the run across Canada. It's a real miracle. Of course, I was in constant pain the whole time, I spent six months in recovery, and my hips hurt until the following spring, but during the crossing itself, I never suffered an injury that forced me to stop.

All runners suffer injuries, myself included. In fact, the recent popularity of running and other types of physical exercise has resulted in overcrowded sports medicine and physiotherapy clinics. I started training for triathlons in 2009 and devoted myself body and soul to them for several years. The sport quickly became a drug for me. Physical activity became a way of life;

I set ambitious goals and surrounded myself with people who shared the same passion. I was driven by a need to challenge myself, and that fire was burning brightly within me.

I progressed quickly, even edging close to the qualifications for the Ironman World Championship in Kona, Hawaii. However, my first seasons were marred by several injuries. Also, although the triathlon consists of three endurance tests (swimming, cycling, and running), all my injuries occurred in the running portion.

My journey across Canada required years of planning. Major sponsors funded the project, and I was under enormous pressure. Questions about injuries surfaced frequently in my meetings with sponsors. We all had to recognize that injuries were possible and that we would have to manage them when they occurred, according to their severity. It was a throw of the dice.

The first months were critical. I ran less at the beginning to allow my body to acclimate. Slowly, my body adapted and learned more skills. In my mind, however, I told myself that it was only a matter of time before I would suffer an injury.

Weeks and months passed, and the injuries that I feared the most never occurred. I ran at my own pace, some days more quickly than others. It was not a test of speed: the only thing that mattered was that I ran 40 kilometres every day. In four hours if possible, in six hours if necessary; no one was judging me. All I wanted was to reach Vancouver on schedule. The pace was my own. Very rarely, the reasons my brain offered at the 38th kilometre were valid. When they were, I listened to them and I no doubt avoided injury by doing so. The line is thin: persevere, persist at the 38th kilometre of the challenge, or stop to protect the goal. Remember the elastic band, which can be played with forever, but that will only break once.

A few months after the campaign, after a well-deserved break, I returned to my old passions: triathlons, intense training, and performance. It was also a return to injury.

I couldn't understand it. I had run five or six marathons per week for nine months without injuring myself even once. I was doing triathlons again, diversifying my disciplines, training for a modest 15 hours per week, and yet I was injuring myself. Was it a mystery? Not really.

I think we all have a certain rhythm written into our DNA, literally and figuratively. The rhythm is not limited to running, but extends to everything we do, to every part of our lives. It belongs to us and defines us. It's who we are. Since my run across Canada was not a question of speed, I was able to listen to and follow my own rhythm. As soon as I started competing again, my need to succeed forced me to break from my rhythm, and that's when the problems surfaced.

The problem is that we never feel that our rhythm is good enough or fast enough. Social pressures, false ideas about success, or an incorrect value scale make us feel inadequate. Our neighbour always seems better, faster, and happier. Seeing that, we increase our rhythm and end up exhausting ourselves and injuring ourselves personally, professionally, and emotionally. In truth, our rhythm, whatever it is, is perfectly acceptable. By respecting it, we can go much further and much faster than if we try to go 200 kilometres per hour, only to hit a wall and find ourselves immobilized for months on end.

During my run across Canada, I found my rhythm, a zone where I could play with the elastic band forever. By following it, I crossed the country with a smile, one step at a time. Finding your rhythm is relatively simple. I even suspect that we all already know it. The real challenge is to accept it and follow it. This is a humbling experience for most of us. In fact, very few people these days respect their own rhythm. Everything seems to indicate that our rhythm is not enough, and our careers demand more and more of us every day. We don't want to end up behind others or be considered the losers. So we speed up the pace, compete with others who themselves are speeding up, all of us afraid of losing. Eventually, participants collapse one after the other, often before anyone reaches the finish line. Worse, and unfortunately too often, we commit to this mad dash, which is counterproductive and inconsistent, only to direct ourselves towards the wrong finish line.

At your own rhythm, you are tireless. One step at a time, by following your own rhythm, you will guarantee your dreams and your goals, regardless of your quest, provided that you can be patient. Of course, people will outpace you from time to time. This is normal and, above all, unimportant. In turn, you'll overtake others, which is also unimportant if you've found your own motivation, or your why. One step at a time, at your own pace, you will go wherever you want.

Butterflies

After having climbed between Camps 1, 2, and 3 several times on Everest, we returned to Base Camp once again, seeking rest and acclimatization. Feverish excitement began to take hold in Base Camp, a multicoloured village of red, yellow, green, and blue tents. The goal was within reach, and every team was planning their final climb to the summit. With the first attempts to reach the summit also come the first deaths. After their attempt, climbers return to Base Camp one after the other, most on their own two legs, but some are brought down in their sleeping bags. Some will appear disappointed, while others will be lit up with infinite joy.

Before we could join the parade, one last logical step had to be taken: a descent to an even lower altitude, to Pheriche at 4,200 metres, a thousand metres below Base Camp. This step is taken to rest and gather energy, since we'll need every last drop on the climb. It's fascinating to feel what a difference a thousand metres makes on breathing. After you've spent several weeks in high altitudes, descending 1,000 metres makes the air feel tangible, as though you could hold it in your hand. Breathing becomes easy and efficient, your appetite returns, and sleep is easier. This stay is essential for recharging our batteries completely before attempting the main event.

Pheriche does not have the same flavour as Namche Bazaar, but it's no less spectacular. Nestled on the edge of a long plain between mountains that seem small compared to the nearby giants, the village is made up of about 20 houses. These homes are masonry masterpieces, each piece cut by hand from raw stone. It's a long and arduous task, and the sound of a mallet striking stone was constant on each of my three visits to the region. Each lot is marked by a fence, also made of stone. The tree line stops at just below 4,000 metres, leaving the village completely exposed with only the barest ground vegetation.

We spent our days reading and discussing our strategy. We also reviewed potential emergency situations and various decisions we might be forced to make, as well as their underlying scenarios.

I kept a journal on my website during the whole process of the climb. Once or twice per week, I left a voicemail message for a friend via satellite phone so that he could update my website with the latest news. The internet had made its debut in the region, including at Pheriche. Powered by solar panels and a generator, one of the buildings had a few computers and an internet connection that allowed us to read some email, when the satellite cooperated.

With good luck, I would soon to be the first Canadian with type 1 diabetes to reach the summit of Everest, and the third person with diabetes in the world to accomplish that feat. The project made a huge splash in the Canadian diabetic community, which unfortunately numbers more than three million people, types 1 and 2 combined. Note that only 10 percent of people with diabetes have type 1 diabetes. It is the more serious form of the condition, and cannot be prevented or cured. Type 2 diabetes is attributed to poor lifestyle and can be prevented or at least delayed by a healthy diet and regular exercise. I was therefore receiving an impressive number of encouraging emails at the time. One of them was from a mother.

I will never forget her email. She wished me the best of luck and confided that her teenage daughter had also had type 1 diabetes. God knows that being different is extremely difficult in adolescence. Her daughter had always hated her condition and refused to accept it. At the worst point in her crisis, revolting against her condition, she decided to stop taking her insulin shots, and died a few days later. Sadly, the diabetes community loses a few adolescents every week this way.

Her mother told me that the wound was still raw, that she would have given anything for her daughter to see things differently. She wished me a safe climb and return, well aware of the positive impact the accomplishment could have on young people. I was particularly stunned by this email. This woman was telling me about her daughter's view of life, about the black lens through which she had viewed her condition.

At the other end of the world, everything around me was sublime: the valley, the mountains, the river flowing down the mountainside, the flowers on the ground. Just a year earlier, I had been in this exact spot with 10 teens with type 1 diabetes, whom I had guided all the way to Everest Base Camp, a trek we had undertaken to raise funds for diabetes research. The trek to Base Camp is extremely difficult. One hiker in five doesn't make it. My group of young people with diabetes all succeeded, leaving behind one of our chaperones, a healthy adult.

A year later, glued to the screen, my state of mind was quite different. When one of our peers suffers, we suffer with them. I was feeling a lot of sadness, frustration, and powerlessness.

I dearly wished that the girl could have seen things differently. I felt the need to withdraw for a moment, to empty my mind, to try to understand. I laced up my hiking boots and headed out. I took a trail and walked slowly for about an hour before finding a small summit that overlooked the village. Here, I stopped to think about this young girl, her life, and the end she had chosen. I was surrounded by beauty worthy of a postcard. The words her mother had written to me echoed in my mind: *I wish she could have seen life and her obstacle differently.* I wish that this young girl could have sat there with me, and that she could have seen how beautiful things can be.

I stayed there for a long time, breathing calmly, my eyes shut, meditating on what I would have liked that girl to have seen. I was trying to lend her my eyes, symbolically. When I opened my eyes, I saw a flight of white butterflies. At 4,200 metres above sea level, it seemed a little strange, but I remembered that butterflies are a symbol of transformation and transition. It was as though the girl had seen them and she was telling me through this sign that after the irreparable had happened, she was finally accepting the condition, and the weight of her struggle had finally been lifted.

My feelings of frustration and sadness dissipated. I returned to camp. A few days later, we returned to Base Camp, a thousand metres higher. We had arrived in Nepal on March 24, and it was now mid-May. Fully charged, our bodies and minds acclimated and well rested, our climb towards the summit was upon us. Everything was about to begin.

Joy

It's happened twice: the first time was in Kyrgyzstan in 2006, during my first climb above 7,000 metres, and the second time was in Tibet in 2007, on Cho Oyu (8,202 metres), the sixth-highest mountain in the world. Each time, everything began with a roar, a vibration deep in the glacier. Then, I heard shouting. I looked up and saw something terrifying: an avalanche bearing down on us, a powerful white cloud, as majestic as it was devastating. In a flash, the conviction that death is imminent takes over. From a distance, a white mass seems to devour the flank of the mountain, slowly and almost gracefully. In reality, the deadly mass rushes down the mountain at tens of metres per second, ruthless, blind, merciless. Rendered powerless and frozen in place, I thought each time that I would be dead in the coming seconds.

Lenin Peak, Kyrgyzstan, Fall 2006

The day started like any other. I was climbing with a Greek team, and the expedition had so far proven to be extremely demanding. The Russian team responsible for logistics had fallen short on every aspect. All the food provided for the five weeks of the expedition was stale, and nearly the whole team had been struck with gastroenteritis. Of nine climbers who had started this expedition, we had become just two, led by our Russian guide.

I lost over 20 pounds during that expedition. To avoid falling ill, I decided not to eat any of the food provided by the logistics team, a risky choice given my type 1 diabetes and the effort required for the climb. Fortunately, I had brought a bag of granola bars, juice powders, and sweets designed to treat potential hypoglycemia. Because of these rations, I was able to ingest a few calories each day and carry on. Ironically, it's thanks to my diabetes that I was able to continue the expedition.

We left Camp 1 to climb to the next camp and acclimatize to the altitude. A few other teams were already high up in the mountain at 5,000 metres above sea level. It was a sunny day, we were making steady progress, and conditions seemed favourable. Meanwhile, we were about 3,500 metres above sea level, busy crossing a field of crevices that required our full concentration. The season had seen little snow, which meant the crevices were exposed, making our task easier.

It was then that I felt the roar and the vibrations. I looked up. Two thousand metres above us, part of the snowy slab had separated from the mountain. Panic struck instantly. The avalanche was quickly gaining in size and speed, and we were right in its path. For the first time in my life, I felt absolute certainty that I would stay there, and that my death was imminent. It's a powerful feeling, difficult to explain and impossible to reproduce. It's terrifying, chilling, sad, and frustrating all at the same time. Your heart races, pounding in your chest. Why me, why now? I was shaking. Pinned between crevices, there was nowhere to hide and nowhere to run. We were completely exposed. Blocks of ice began to fly past like comets on either side of us. Some were the size of basketballs, others were much larger. Just one of those projectiles could have torn us apart. We lay down on the ground and waited in silence for death to take us.

Cho Oyu, Tibet, November 2007

In anticipation of our Everest climb the following year, Rob, Wayne, Eric, Darrell, our guides, and I were training on Cho Oyu in Tibet. On their own, journeys to these faraway lands transform and shape us. We had the opportunity to climb together a lot in British Columbia, where we all lived, except for Wayne who was from California. At 8,202 metres above sea level, this mountain commands respect. Just 600 metres lower than Everest, Cho Oyu is essentially the same climb with the same amount of risk, but without the glory of having conquered the mountain that captivates the imagination.

Tibet is a fascinating land. We were there in November, and the journey to the mountain was an adventure all its own. From home, I once again headed to Kathmandu. We packed all our equipment into several 4x4s, and the Sherpa team also took a few vehicles. Our procession then took the road north to cross the Tibetan border. Landslides had damaged the roads, so we had to cross a few rivers. The vehicle I shared with Rob was almost washed away by the flooding, which gave us a good scare. The journey took us through a green rainforest in the mountains, then across windy and rocky desert plains. With every kilometre travelled, the temperature dropped while the altitude increased. The Himalayan giants watched us from a distance.

We had barely gotten set up at Base Camp when Rob had to leave the mountain due to infection. Later during the expedition, one of our guides, John Furneaux, suffered a pulmonary edema while we were at Camp 1. Given the urgency, he asked us to help him descend back to Base Camp. It was the middle of the night. The expedition was already going poorly, and we had just reached Camp 1 with a lot of work. We were each resting in our own tents when John asked if one of us wanted to descend with him. I remember the moment of silence that followed. After a few seconds, I offered to go. We quickly organized the descent. Once it began, in complete darkness, John and I realized that his state was much more serious than we had thought. Halfway down, John had to stop.

I left him my sleeping bag in addition to his own. John would have to stay resting on the mountain in the middle of the night to conserve his energy and control his breathing. Meanwhile, I had to descend as quickly as I could, but also as cautiously as possible, in order to find help. When I left John, he turned off his headlamp. He would turn it back on when the rescue team arrived so that they could find him, in approximately five hours.

Our roles had changed. John was no longer our guide. He would now have to trust the team. This story contains many elements of leadership that I discuss in my talks to companies. Making tough decisions, defining and switching roles, and sharing power; in short, the mountain never stops teaching. My role at that moment was not to be a hero. All I had to do was reach Base Camp. I gave everything I could and drained my energy stores to arrive as quickly as possible without taking pointless risks that would have only made the situation worse. On the mountain and in companies, we carry a torch that belongs not to one person, but to the whole team. My role on that night was to carry the torch for the team that would make the climb in search of John.

John survived his night on the mountain side and, a few days later, we were able to have him evacuated. The following year on Everest, it was thanks to him that I came back in one piece.

The poor weather that had raged during the early part of the expedition had kept all the teams at Base Camp for an eternity. After a bumpy start, the remaining team members were eager to get underway. The window to make the climb had shortened considerably, and after a few days in the higher altitudes, it was now or never. Armed with our courage, we left Base Camp on a sunny morning to try to reach Camp 1. Some 10 hours of work awaited us.

Halfway up, I felt a rumble and a vibration in the ground that I knew only too well. Then came the screams and the panic. Porters and Sherpa ran in every direction, completely terrified. You know it's serious when the Sherpa are panicking. It was a massive avalanche. Three thousand metres above us, the white cloud seemed to be descending towards us in slow motion, an elegant, domineering, cruel, imperious, powerful white mass. Once again, it was right upon us, with no obstacle to slow it down. Like the Sherpa, I tried to flee. My heart immediately started pounding in my chest, and the altitude was certainly not helping. I lay down behind a boulder the size of a washing machine and covered my head with my backpack to try to create an air pocket. A light dusting of powder snow covered us, announcing the avalanche that was just seconds from hitting us. I waited, convinced that I would die in the next few seconds. For the second time in my life, I was living the same nightmare.

In each case, the avalanche miraculously stopped a little higher than I was. On Lenin Peak, none of us was struck by the massive ice pieces tumbling down the mountain. On Cho Oyu, the whole avalanche was immobilized on a plateau a thousand metres above us.

What follows this unlikely survival is extraordinary. Everyone reacts differently. Some burst into laughter, others start to cry, and still others will shout their gratitude at the top of their lungs. Your knees buckle, your heart races, and your hands shake.

When I realized that I had survived, I felt an intense explosion of joy, a breathtaking sentiment of happiness, the most intense sense of elation I had ever felt. In chemical terms, a huge dose of adrenaline, endorphins, and dopamine fills the body to create a feeling of indescribable euphoria. It's a rush, not unlike the kind created by certain drugs, but the intensity is a hundred times stronger. It lasts just 10 to 15 seconds. I've never felt anything like it; nothing else has ever been so intense. These two almost mystical experiences changed my life. A door to an unknown world opened, as though I had just discovered the existence of a secret, of a rare and ardent joy, of a trance-like state.

The immense happiness that you feel in these few seconds comes from the simple joy of being alive. Everything else becomes meaningless and futile. Finances, work, relationships, small everyday annoyances, envy, worries, all of it takes a backseat. The joy of being alive is so powerful that nothing else matters. We are bursting with gratitude. In those few seconds, we imagine ourselves living in poverty, missing a limb, or working a monotonous job, and we tell ourselves that none of it would be so bad. The simple joy of being alive is too great. We realize how precious life is, that life itself is beautiful, and that everything else, everything we've built and collected, is a mere accessory to the main event.

I've never forgotten this high, this state, this feeling, this sensation, even though it was triggered by a traumatic event. I hope that everyone can someday live such an experience. It

centres and calms you. It brings you back to basics. It eliminates the stress and the pressure we put on ourselves and
the pressure we mistakenly let others burden us with. Since
no drug is powerful enough to replicate this experience, and
since I have no desire to see another avalanche bear down on
me, I rely on my memories of the mountains. When times are
tough, I revisit those two moments of enlightenment, that joy
and the simple pleasure of being there. They take the stress
out of everything, make me smile, and help me to keep going
on my worst days.

Our pursuit of happiness must be simple and intrinsically
focused. Happiness is a way of waking up; it's not something to
achieve. I'm not always in a good mood, but I am always happy.
Every day, we run a marathon, go to work, work hard to move
forward, to progress, and to enrich ourselves, always while
saying, *if I accomplish this, I'll obtain that*. We want a diploma to
get a good job. We want a good job to make money. We want
money to travel and buy a beautiful house. We want a beautiful
house to live in the best neighbourhood and to be able to say
that we are successful. We want all that to be happy. And
we want to be happy to...? The chain stops there. Once we've
achieved happiness, we can't exchange it for something else.
Nobody has ever said they want to be happy to own a boat.
We want a boat to be happy.

Happiness is a habit, a philosophy—it's a way of living.
It's not a goal or something we obtain, and it's definitely not
something we possess or accumulate. It must not be based on

achieving a goal. American billionaire Mark Cuban said it well in January 2016, when the US Powerball lottery jackpot reached a record of almost two billion dollars: "If you aren't happy today, you won't be happy tomorrow with two billion dollars."

Happiness is a habit, not a goal.

If you had suggested amputating both my legs to save my life in the 10 seconds following each avalanche, I would have gladly agreed. Many recent studies have shown that our living situation accounts for just 10 percent of our happiness. The aspect with the greatest impact on our level of happiness? Our attitude. The key to happiness lies in what we decide to do with what we have, in the courage to change what we can, even if we are born in a slum.

This is the well-known positive attitude. It is often said of athletic success that it's all in your head, that to succeed, you must have mental fortitude. This is true. Most importantly, this strength of mind is not something that a person has or does not have. It's not a character trait. Like a muscle, it is something that is developed. The good news is that a positive attitude is possible for, and accessible to, everyone. I'm not trying to be pretentious when I say that the mental perseverance I needed to be able to run 170 marathons in nine months is both Herculean and extremely rare. This isn't bragging, it's just the facts, an observation. It's also worth noting that 10 years before I ran across Canada, I did not have one hundredth of the mental endurance that I have today. I slowly built it up. I don't have anything special and I'm not more intelligent than the average person. Everyone can, without exception, develop titanic mental strength. All you have to do is devote effort to doing so.

We all possess a certain amount of mental endurance; some are born with a little more or a little less, but it doesn't make a difference. Someone with a small amount of endurance who chooses to work towards increasing it will quickly overtake someone who has a greater natural endurance but who does not make any effort to improving it. I was always chosen last for sports teams in my youth. With patience and a lot of work, I eventually awoke one day at the summit of Everest. Like building muscles, you must be patient. Mental strength does not appear overnight, but it is accessible, attainable, and available for everyone. It also comes one step at a time.

So how do you develop this remarkable mental resilience? By failing and recovering as often as possible. I'll say it again: failure is an ingredient. By choosing to face adversity whenever possible and by forcing ourselves to overcome hardship, we develop mental strength and a positive attitude focused on solutions rather than on problems. It doesn't involve risking our lives or doing something illogical or irrational, of course, but it does involve a constant search for the next logical step to take. I've had so many difficult days in my life that I've developed a belief that regardless of the obstacles, regardless of how hard a day is, I will always win.

Doubt

After many years of preparation, the moment I left to try my luck on Everest was very emotional. My family and friends gathered at the airport, having taken care to arrive early to share a meal together.

When it came time to go through security, I hugged each person in my family tightly. My emotions were all over the place, but I was especially filled with pride and anxiety. My mother was the last to hug me. I will never forget that moment. I saw in her eyes that she knew very well that I might not return.

The feeling of guilt that rose in me was very painful. We train for all kinds of situations that could occur on the mountain, but it's always when we least expect it that we are rendered completely powerless. For the first time in my life, I realized that my choices also impacted those who stayed behind.

I had never felt more guilt in my life. I had made a choice, but the people who loved me were forced to live with that choice. The challenge was imposed upon them, too. What my parents did that day is admirable. They did what was best for the mission, not what was most comfortable to them.

It was then that the promise of returning home became more important than my ambition to succeed. I realized that the summit is only half the journey. Since most deaths on Everest happen on the way down, I had to put my finish line not at the top of the mountain, but at the bottom. Success did not matter so much anymore; the only thing that really counted was coming back in one piece.

In the middle of the night, two months later, I was approaching my goal. Weakened by a very difficult climb from Camp 3 to Camp 4, we decided to stop at Camp 4 (8,000 metres) for 24 hours before trying for the summit. At very high altitudes, the low atmospheric pressure significantly reduces the oxygen levels in the air. The lack of oxygen makes life almost impossible, and as a result, the zone above 8,000 metres is known as the death zone. Even with oxygen cylinders, even with the most sophisticated equipment available, humans can only survive in this zone for a window of about 72 hours.

The perilous final climb to the summit started at eight o'clock at night. We were hoping to reach the summit the next morning and return to Camp 4 by the end of the day. The final push takes almost 24 hours. The plan looked good on paper, but it did not leave us much time in case of the unexpected, a rescue operation, or an accident.

The final climb is surreal. We were wearing high-altitude climbing suits that are resistant to extreme cold, boots and crampons, and bags weighed down with oxygen cylinders. We were equipped with oxygen masks and kept our water bottles close to our bodies. In the dark, broken only by the beams of our headlamps, our pace was slow, but steady. A consistent pace became our best strategy. When we left Camp 4, the moon was rising slowly behind the mountains, throwing light strong enough to cast shadows.

We reached the Balcony at about one in the morning. The Balcony is a prominent landmark located halfway between Camp 4 and the summit. In terms of elevation, it's about 500 metres of added height. In terms of distance, it's barely two kilometres in five hours. The altitude demands respect and patience. At this stage of the climb, we were moving forward at the rate of one step for every five to 10 breaths. If there's a place where you ask yourself what you're doing there, it's definitely here!

The Balcony is followed by a narrow ledge that is about 300 metres long and only a few metres wide. On our left is a 2,000-metre drop to nothing. Via that route, you'd be back in Camp 2 in a few seconds. On the right, another 2,000-metre drop, with China lurking somewhere below.

The night was long, and so was each step, and we had all the time in the world to think. On this ledge, your mind can question anything. Mine meandered to the moment I first met Nicole Johnson, six months earlier.

Nicole Johnson also has type 1 diabetes. In 1999, she was declared Miss America. I met Nicole at a diabetes conference in the US, at which we were both speakers. During the weekend, our mission was to meet young teens with diabetes. Nicole was a hit with them because she had a strong message, filled with hope and possibilities.

To make the meeting as exciting and interactive as possible, I had brought climbing equipment, including the high-altitude winter climbing suit I planned to use on Everest. Nicole put it on to entertain the audience, who found it very funny. We easily won them over. The picture of Nicole, completely swallowed up in my enormous winter climbing suit, is full of contrast and it's very funny.

Months later, in extremely inhospitable conditions, I was slowly advancing along this ridge, dressed in the same climbing suit, when I was struck by a sad realization: the one and only time I had the opportunity to meet a Miss America winner, she was wrapped up in a polar snowsuit thanks to my brilliant idea to undertake a Mount Everest ascent. I'd always imagined that if I were ever to meet a Miss America winner, she would be dressed in something much lighter! I had brought my uniform, so why had she not worn hers?

I like to tell this anecdote as a joke, because it introduces the notion of doubt. Inevitably, doubt arises at a great point of resistance. At more than 8,500 metres above sea level, abandoned to your own thoughts in the dark, when you're alive only thanks to your oxygen mask, you ask yourself a lot of questions. Is the risk worthwhile? Why should I suffer so much pain to achieve something? Why do I even want to achieve self-realization? Is my normal life not enough? Does any of this mean anything? Very few of you will ever climb this ridge, because very few people even go there. However, the feelings we experience there are universal: doubt, fear, questioning, the search for meaning, and the desire to quit, to name just a few. We all experience these feelings. Neither our social status nor our collection of achievements can inoculate us against doubt. Besides being necessary and unavoidable, moments of doubt are valuable, useful, and filled with possibility. We should welcome them, cherish them, and make good use of them. Doubt validates our intentions.

Doubt is a process of validation that reminds us of our why, our motivation, our mission, and our intent. I wanted to use action to show the 420 million people around the world with diabetes that they can lead amazing and fulfilling lives and accomplish their dreams.

It's not about trying to overcome doubt, but about using it to generate energy. We must transform it into a springboard. I was not alone on the ridge; thousands of people were carrying me. What I was doing had little importance in itself, but the meaning behind the steps I was taking one at a time to achieve my goal carried enormous power.

Doubt is a process of validation.

I was at a talk in Orlando a few years later, where I met a man whose daughter with type 1 diabetes had followed the daily updates of my expedition. I'll never forget what he told me. The news that I had reached the summit of Everest spread like wildfire through the diabetic community across North America thanks to social networks. He told me that he heard his daughter jumping for joy in her bedroom. He burst into tears as he recalled that moment. He told me honestly that Everest was not that important to him. It was what the accomplishment meant for his daughter that had so touched him: She developed an unshakable conviction that her condition would not limit her possibilities and that she could dream as much and as big as she wanted to.

That night, when everything was cast into doubt, I held onto the hope that I was making a difference. My intent transformed doubt into conviction, a conviction that my reaching the summit would mean something to thousands of people. Our surroundings were breathtaking. The neighbouring peaks pierced through the thick carpet of clouds two thousand metres below us. The moon had reached its highest point in the sky, and the world was painted in grey and blue. The sound of the air passing through the valves of my oxygen mask set the pace.

Doubt, questioning, and fear are part of a defence mechanism that is deeply rooted within us. The body and mind are designed to adapt and ultimately to survive for as long as possible.

To do this, we use various reflexes and defence mechanisms. They exist to protect us from dangers inherent in our everyday lives.

They are the reason that we stay back from the subway tracks, that we don't touch a hot stove element, and that we don't quit our job on a whim so that we can continue to meet our needs.

We are very familiar with our physical defence mechanisms. For example, in running, when we run slowly, the body adapts and finds its second wind in a relaxed pace that does not threaten it. However, when we go beyond our abilities, our heart rate increases and our breathing becomes more laboured. The body tries to carry more oxygen to the muscles somehow, but also sends very strong signals through pain and shortness of breath. It signals that we must slow down, that our pace is dangerous, risky, and too fast. We have all experienced this, whether while running or while engaging in another type of physical activity.

I have noticed that we have a much poorer understanding of our emotional defence mechanisms. They take many forms in our attempts to protect ourselves from emotional pain, regret, and disappointment. Doubt and fear of failure are common triggers of these mechanisms. It's the little voice that says *when I'm ready*. It's the decision not to start your own business for fear that it won't work out. It's waiting to be sure before booking a plane ticket for a trip that excites you. It's staying in a loveless relationship to avoid losing everything.

It's not signing up for your first triathlon "for fear of looking foolish". All of these actions are to avoid pain, failure, loneliness, and ridicule.

Our small inner voice is a manifestation of our fear of failure, our fear of the unknown, or whatever else you want to call it. In reality, it is our desire for safety speaking to us, a defence mechanism activating to protect us. Physical or emotional, these defence mechanisms exist for a reason. They are essential, they keep us alive, and they sometimes help us make better decisions. Sometimes, but not all the time.

At other times, it is critical to know how to circumvent them. I've discussed this extensively. Choosing to face an obstacle and the resistance it creates is the only way to grow and develop to your full potential. Circumventing a defence mechanism involves changing your internal monologue, sort of like changing the channel on a radio.

Consider the following scenario. Your employer wants to send you to the other end of the world for work. The opportunity is quite interesting, but change and fear of the unknown are making you hesitate. Now imagine a radio representing your inner voice, which you can tune to one of two frequencies. On one frequency, you pick up message number one, and on the other, message number two.

Frequency 1:   I'm succeeding here, why go there and risk failing? Why should I start from scratch? What if it doesn't work out? What's more, I don't know anyone in that city. Will I be able to perform well?

Frequency 2:   New friendships are waiting for me there. I have the support of my family and friends, who want to see me progress and who will still be here when I return. The experience will undoubtedly propel my career forward. I will meet people who will broaden my horizons. What an amazing opportunity for growth and learning!

These two messages are very different. Does the first reflect reality? Not at all! It's just a defence mechanism. The problem is that we're concerned for our safety, so our internal radio is often set to the first frequency. If this can reassure you, know that's normal and genetic.

During my run across Canada, I had hours upon hours of time to reflect every day. I noticed that my thoughts had a natural tilt towards the negative. This seems to be true for most of us. Intrigued by this sad reality, I asked a psychologist about it. Why do humans naturally turn towards more negative thoughts? The reason is simple. The guilty party? Our survival instinct. To survive, our brain is programmed to anticipate the worst-case scenario and protect us from it. This instinct has been written into our DNA since lion attacks, lack of food, and neighbouring tribes were major threats. Today, most real threats have disappeared, but the instinct is still present.

We are not obliged to believe and obey the first message. In our professional and personal lives, we must make a conscious effort to change the frequency of our internal radio.

Simply understanding that it is a defence mechanism is winning half the battle. We often mistake our fears for reality, but they are nothing more than a scene orchestrated by our brains to prevent us from moving forward. Once we realize this, we can respond more appropriately. We can choose to circumvent this defence mechanism and choose the option that is difficult and uncomfortable but that also offers an enormous potential for growth.

What I have realized is that, unlike physical defence mechanisms, which are mostly innate, emotional defence mechanisms are largely acquired. Acquired from whom? Acquired from what? Were they imposed upon us? Are they appropriate? Do they work? Are they fixed or changing? One thing is certain: our emotional defence mechanisms are always comfortable. However, comfortable does not equal effective, logical, or a promise of growth.

Someone whose partner commits adultery will tend to protect themselves emotionally afterwards by being mistrustful in future relationships. That instinct was acquired from a previous experience. However, mistrust is perhaps not the best way to grow or even build a new relationship. The emotional defence mechanism (in this case, mistrust) must be circumvented to allow a new relationship to fully flourish.

Let's look at another example: my relationship with money. I grew up in a very traditional family. We were devout and practising Catholics. As a child, I was often told that I had to work hard, and that money was earned with difficulty. I was told that rich people were dishonest and corrupt. I was also told that life is hard and that we earn our place in heaven through suffering. When I was 12 years old, I started my first summer job on a farm. I was earning three dollars per hour and I had never worked so hard in my whole life. My siblings and I had incredible parents. They passed on the values of hard work and perseverance, which allowed us to accomplish great things, and we owe much of our success to the way they raised us.

This being said, at the beginning of my 30s, I saw several of my friends beginning to accumulate wealth and property. I did not share this financial success. Worse, many of those friends were becoming richer without too much effort. I felt envy and frustration because of that fact. It was by reading T. Harv Eker's book, *Secrets of the Millionaire Mind*, that I became aware of one of my most debilitating defence mechanisms. I highly recommend the book. Subconsciously, financial success was something unclean to me, something that I thought would make me a crook. My defence mechanism to avoid becoming a bad person was therefore to remain poor. I had also been programmed to believe that money does not grow on trees. My jobs and projects had proven that: everything had to be difficult, and nothing came easily to me. To change things,

I had to become aware of this defence mechanism, observe it, and understand it. Next I consciously and voluntarily tried uncomfortable and counterintuitive behaviours to make a change that would help me to move forward.

Trying out new and different behaviours, what an interesting concept.

We try on clothes in a store to see whether they fit us and how we like them. Occasionally, we try on clothes that are completely different from our usual style and from what we're used to wearing. Sometimes we don't even leave the dressing room to show our companion, but from time to time, we surprise ourselves. We dare to try a different style and come out of the dressing room, proud of our new look, and we adopt it as our own.

We work to correct our flaws, improve ourselves, evolve, and grow. This idea loses meaning when it is overused. Instead of working to correct your flaws, have you considered trying new behaviours? Just once, just to see? Working at your flaws is a long, tedious, and, honestly, depressing process. Whether or not we're willing to admit it, we normally know our own flaws: we're impatient, angry, jealous, self-centred, hostile to change, pretentious, or lazy, to name just a few!

Trying a new behaviour leads to a more positive experience instead of shining a spotlight on what we do badly. What's more, trying does not mean you have to commit to anything, and it's often easy. This technique also carries no risk. In the worst-case scenario, we can try the new behaviour once and go back to our old habits if it doesn't suit us. But trust in my experience, because often, we surprise ourselves when we realize that the new behaviour works for us and creates a sense of well-being, so we try it again and gradually adopt it as our own. It's like our wardrobe: we don't change all our clothing at once. It's by trying new behaviours that we find the things we like, and it's with time that we improve ourselves.

To circumvent my defence mechanism, I had to try out new behaviours and change my beliefs. I had to try to believe that money was not necessarily difficult to earn. Through different strategies and tricks, for example by developing passive income streams, I've come to believe that it can be easy to earn money. I also chose to be paid based on the value of what I offer and not based on hours worked. I forced myself to meet rich people and build a relationship with them. These new behaviours allowed me to rethink my relationship with money over time, to enjoy a wonderful quality of life and balance in my life, and to increase my income.

The Rockies

I crossed into Manitoba on August 9, 2014, some 4,500 kilometres, 110 marathons, and six months after I had left Newfoundland and Labrador. Up until that point, the road had been winding and rarely went in a straight line. I could cover 40 kilometres in one day, but I was always twisting north or south. I was definitely moving towards my goal, but on the scale of the whole of Canada, my progress was quite slow. After crossing the border out of Ontario, the speed at which I was moving westwards sharply increased.

Just steps into Manitoba, the road became a straight line, headed all the way to the Rockies so 40 kilometres of running now meant 40 kilometres towards the west. I had to run 500 kilometres to cross Manitoba, 660 to cross Saskatchewan, and just 370 to cross Alberta. Moving over 200 kilometres per week, I quickly traversed the Prairies.

From Winnipeg, I followed the Trans-Canada Highway to Medicine Hat, Alberta. The Trans-Canada Highway was the most logical road, both legally accessible to runners and reasonably safe, although a bit busy and noisy. From Medicine Hat, I chose to follow Highway 3, known as Crowsnest Highway, a winding road that leads all the way to Hope, British Columbia, before undertaking the final leg, a 200-kilometre descent to Vancouver. After months of working out all the kinks, our logistics were now a well-oiled machine. Patrick and I had our own habits, had learned to understand each other, listen to each other, and let each other do our own jobs. There was no hierarchy; I might have signed the cheques, but I wasn't the boss. Without each other, we were nothing.

The months of running had left their mark on me. I had lost weight and was suffering from incredible mental fatigue. The pain, a constant in my life for six months, had become normal. I was used to struggling to get up out of a chair, to being constantly exhausted, to feeling pain in my legs every morning, afternoon, and night. The fact that it was such a constant reduced the pain a little. I had forgotten what life was like before the pain. My appetite had decreased. The more we practise something, the more efficient we become at it, and the more our bodies follow that principle. Since my body had become more efficient in producing and storing energy, I did not need to absorb as many calories. An amusing aside: I finished my run across Canada in mid-November. I took a well-deserved break, followed immediately by Christmas. Suddenly, I stopped burning 6,000 calories per day and started eating much more. And what happened? One month after having finished the last marathon of my journey, I had developed a soft belly!

Recognizing the opportunity we had, Patrick and I became increasingly attached to our lifestyle. We liked the trailer a lot. We had arranged it according to our needs, adding some comfort, personal effects, and useful items. It was our home. Time was still moving forward, and without warning, fall was at the door. The fourth and final season was beginning; four seasons experienced while running or in the cabin of a truck, calmly, one step at a time, one turn of the wheel at a time, one kilometre at a time. I remember the first snowfall that autumn.

It was barely snowing, just a few timid snowflakes, the sort of October snow that does not stick to the ground, a mini-blizzard lit by rays of sunlight. It was a weak snowfall, but very symbolic; I stopped to stare at it in wonder, as though it were my first time seeing snow, my hands stretched out in front of me to catch the snowflakes. I was shocked to realize that we had started this journey a long time ago, and I had been running for a long time. We had experienced every kind of intense weather over almost a year, and the snowflakes brought a simple message with them. Soon it would be time to go home, and everything would end.

It was when I was at my most physically exhausted that the Rockies began to rise on the horizon. Reaching the British Columbia border was a great victory for me. Although I was still a thousand kilometres from Vancouver, I had crossed the borders of each province. Whatever would happen from this moment on, the road had been long enough to grant meaning to the action. Even if something unforeseen or a severe injury forced me to stop 300 kilometres from Vancouver, the road travelled had been long enough to send a powerful message.

Eight hundred of the thousand kilometres left to run were in the Rockies. With all its climbs, this segment alone represented a total 30,000 metres in altitude gained, the equivalent of almost three and a half Everest climbs, which I would have to make in the last month of the campaign.

British Columbia offers breathtaking landscapes. Patrick was like a kid in a candy store: he spent a lot of time taking pictures.

The Okanagan Valley is beautiful in October. However, for each small, picturesque village nestled at the bottom of the valley, with its quaint fruit and vegetable stands, there was always a steep climb the next day. While the landscape was magnificent, the physical effort demanded by the mountains was brutal. I had to cross several passes, including Kootenay Pass, a total climb of 37 kilometres, peaking at nearly 1,800 metres above sea level. This was without a doubt one of the hardest days of the campaign. It took me seven and a half hours to reach the summit, switching between walking and running. The next day, the descent over the same distance finished off what the climb had started. My legs were like jelly. My calves and glutes were on fire from the climb. The descent focused on my quadriceps, as though the mountain had a whole strategy dedicated to ridding itself of runners.

My motivation, at least, escaped unharmed. More than ever, I was connected to my why, my intention, my mission. And because of this unity with my mission, I was able to resist the temptation of celebrating too early. I was working, and I had to continue with the same concentration, the same determination, and the same precision as I had in the first months. For the mission and to highlight my message, I wanted a grand arrival in Vancouver. My partners, sponsors, film crew, public relations team, and everyone else were planning for my arrival in Vancouver.

The week of my arrival in the city was one of the best of my life. My parents surprised me there, especially considering how much they hate flying. My brother, who also has type 1 diabetes, and my sister were also there. Even the weather was nice, which was extremely lucky for mid-November, and the ideal scenario for our arrival. World Diabetes Day is observed on November 14 around the world. From day one of campaign planning, two years earlier, my target was clear: I wanted to finish the adventure on that day. Thanks to Patrick's great calculations and lots of perseverance on my part, we arrived on time.

We established our base camp for the week, this time in Vancouver. Each morning, as we had done religiously up until then, we left the trailer to go back to where I had stopped the day before and I ran 40 kilometres westwards, returning to Vancouver in the evening.

The whole week was all about symbolism. Obviously, I would not "arrive" in Vancouver on November 14th, since we were already there, Patrick having set up our base camp for the last 10 days there for obvious logistical reasons.

Most of the media attention I would receive would be at the very end. I was already feeling incredibly emotional. Did I feel like I had succeeded? Not quite. Only a few days of running remained, and we had already visited the arrival site many times, but I didn't feel like we could celebrate just yet. I have a vivid memory of running some 100 kilometres outside Vancouver, telling myself that I had to stay focused. I didn't want to lower my guard; the thousands of kilometres I had run did not grant me an irrevocable right to the joy of the finish line. Whether I had five or 200 kilometres left, I had to earn each one. I approached the last 100 kilometres the same way I had approached the first 100. I felt the need to put the petal to the metal. It was now or never. It was at that exact moment that we had to work our hardest. Admittedly, my attitude drove Patrick up a wall.

As we approach our goal, our task becomes more difficult, and we must be more focused than ever.

We knocked out each kilometre, one by one. We had to give our exact arrival time to the media, so on the morning of November 14, I ran just a few kilometres. In reality, my run across Canada had ended the day before. I had run the last 40 kilometres and joined my family on the edge of the Pacific, at English Bay. It was a calm and peaceful moment, I was surrounded by my loved ones, and I had succeeded at last. I wanted to experience that moment with my family.

After nine months of running, November 14, 2014, finally arrived. It was the big day and I was ready.

I started giving interviews at 4 o'clock that morning for breakfast television programs on the east coast. My arrival was scheduled for 10 a.m., which we had chosen so that east coast media could announce the news in the evening reports. I had planned to run five symbolic kilometres, both to warm up for my big arrival and to arrive on time. To make sure we had a big crowd and good media coverage, we mobilized a whole school to come to the site. Two weeks earlier, I had gone to that school to give a talk, which was a great success and, of course, the perfect way to generate buzz around my arrival. The students had made banners for the big day, and their genuine energy had a huge impact on me. We chose Second Beach as the site of my arrival, right on the edge of the Pacific and just five minutes from downtown, making it easily accessible to Vancouverites, who awaited us in great numbers. Patrick had acted flawlessly to obtain various permits from the city, and he was responsible for managing the event.

It was hosted by my good friend Shawn Shepheard, who also has type 1 diabetes, and who probably promoted me more than anyone else on social networks during my nine months of running. Music, clearly identified vehicles, a team of volunteers, the public relations firm, the film crew, the tent for the media, the crowd, everything was ready.

Jack Poisson, who had surprised me the day before with his family, joined me for the run. A few hundred metres from the beach, Jack went to join the crowd while I sat down on a rock, waiting to get the text from Patrick to let me know it was time to take the final steps.

I was alone on that rock, emotional but calm. I contemplated the horizon and the Pacific Ocean in silence for a long time. It was here that everything would end. Part of me did not want it to end; I enjoyed our routine, but I was also ready to finally go home. I wondered how I would react at the finish line. I thought back on the thousands of kilometres I had run, on all the effort I had given, on all the people I had met, and on all the memories we would take with us. I was hoping that the project would have a second life after the finish line. I knew the campaign had changed many lives and inspired many people. I was serene. What I had done was not important. The purpose of my journey, its meaning, made me happy.

Moments later, I received Patrick's text. Nearly four hundred people were waiting for me on the beach. As I slowly approached, I could hear the roar of the crowd. There was magic in the air. I saw the arrival site appear on the horizon, and the crowd had formed a long corridor to the ocean. I advanced slowly along this path, hugging many friends tightly, waving to children as I passed, and finally, I stepped into the Pacific.

That moment will stay with me for the rest of my life. Finish lines have a special power to make us forget the pain and transform it into joy. I gave more than 20 interviews and celebrated the accomplishment with Patrick, who deserves half the credit.

The Last Step

From the Balcony, we still had some eight hours to go before we would reach the summit of Mount Everest. The night was long and difficult. We reached the famous Hillary Step at about 7 a.m. At 8,790 metres above sea level, this hundred-metre section is one of the most technical parts of the Everest climb. Some sections are not even 50 centimetres wide, with a sharp plunge to your death on either side. Breathing here is extremely difficult and requires an astounding amount of effort. One year after our misadventure in Tibet, John Furneaux, my guide, paid me back in kind. I was in a state of extreme fatigue, and it was only thanks to his kindness that I was able to cross the Hillary Step without peril.

At around 9 o'clock on May 25, 2008, I stood on the top of Mount Everest. I had kept the promise I had made to myself in 2001. At the summit, I shed a tear and congratulated the entire team. Then, I sat down and contemplated the view as calmly as I could, considering the intensity of that moment and that place. I was on the roof of the world, the summit of Mount Everest, sitting side by side with my biggest dream.

I remember feeling incredible joy on the summit, and I knew very well what it meant. I was exhausted, and everything happened very quickly. At the risk of repeating myself, the summit of Mount Everest is only the halfway point on this journey, not the finish line. Most deaths on Everest occur on the way down. I had been warned about it, but now I was there.

I had reached the summit a few minutes earlier and I was already back to work. I had to descend in one piece.

It took just three days to reach the foot of the mountain. I felt the greatest sense of accomplishment when I arrived at Base Camp. I remember that moment much more clearly than I remember the summit. The joy I felt was also far greater. I had succeeded.

I've been asked one question hundreds of times, and am still being asked it even now: How does it feel when you achieve your greatest dream? How do you feel when everything is finished?

In fact, everything that I had dreamed of accomplishing had begun when I reached the summit. Everything was very far from being over. My motivation, the all-important why at the heart of my actions, is always greater than the accomplishment itself. It transcends borders and summits, and must resonate before, during, and after the achievement. On the mountain, in a company, and in everyday life, it's not about the heights we climb to, but how many people we carry with us. By looking at it this way, summits and finish lines become springboards that propel us to the next phase, the next logical step, which involves making the project useful to others. Leaders are those people who work to make others better.

As I arrived in Vancouver after a run of exactly 7,158 kilometres, the saga of a lifetime was ending. I was eager to return home, rest, and especially to launch the next phase of the project: a book, a film, talks at companies, and so on. I was excited and I never had the impression that Vancouver was the end of the project. The best way to combat the *going-home blues* is to make sure that the project does not end. You can inoculate yourself against the *going-home blues* at the beginning of a project with a strong why.

All my life, I had dreamed of climbing Everest. I had prepared myself for a decade. It took me two months to climb the mountain. I stayed at the peak for just five minutes. *Three hundred seconds!* Faced with this irony, the big lesson we can take away is that success is not a goal, but a consequence. Success is what we get when we target a clear destination, from which we welcome setbacks as teachings, and which we chase after, one step at a time.

Success is not a goal, it is a consequence.

How does the boy always chosen last for a team wake up one day on the summit of Everest? Forget the summit and simply go through your day the best you can. Forget the summit and concentrate instead on acquiring new habits for growth.

Of course, the final step, the destination, or the goal must be clear, but setting goals is not so difficult. You can make a list of goals you want to achieve in just a few seconds and put it up wherever you want. The road to achieve those goals, however, that's another matter altogether. To reach a goal, you must sometimes forget about it and focus on the road or process that will take you there. You must forget the final goal and focus on building simple, day-to-day habits for growth, which are aligned with the goal or mission, and practise them with dedication, discipline, and perseverance.

> Forget the summit.
> Concentrate on acquiring habits for growth.

Positive actions or habits for growth? Actions must be clearly distinguished from habits. Exercise, reading, saving money, drinking less, asking advice from a mentor, working on a project: these are all what I call positive actions.

We all have moments of inspiration where we decide to do something positive. However, without repeating them, they are only isolated acts. They are not without value, but small actions hold no power if they are not repeated.

> A habit for growth is the diligent repetition
> of positive actions that are aligned
> with our mission and our goals.

You must have a strategy and dedicate effort to making a positive act a habit. It's okay to start small. My father always told me not to be afraid of humble beginnings.

Do 20 minutes of exercise four times a week, 15 minutes of reading every night, put $50 aside every week, avoid alcohol from Monday to Thursday, talk to a mentor once a month, dedicate an hour each weekend to working on a personal project: these are all habits for growth. When positive actions are isolated or not repeated, they have a limited impact on our lives. When they are repeated, they become habits for growth with incredible power.

Acquiring habits for growth can restore part of the meaning to the old saying, "anything is possible".

Remember, not everything is possible. I cannot roller skate on the moon. And even with all the determination in the world, a double amputee could never play in the National Hockey League. I'm sorry, but it's just not possible. Although no one should be expected to achieve the impossible, we should still aspire to it at our full potential.

Once acquired and maintained, our habits for growth will contribute to our own transformation. They allow us to realize that we are mentally, physically, and intellectually malleable, that our abilities are not set in stone, that they can grow and diversify. And it's exactly at that moment that the magic happens.

By understanding that our abilities are malleable, we can increase our abilities and grow. We start to define what is possible based on not only what we are today, but also what we could be in the future, and almost everything becomes possible as a result.

> Include a future version of you when
> you define what is possible.

Some goals seem impossible to achieve, but only because we don't yet have the tools or abilities required to achieve them. We've all said it at one time or another: *If only I knew 20 years ago what I know now!* Why not do the opposite and say: *Here is what I'll be able to do in 20 years with all the skills I will have acquired.*

Experiencing the final step in the Sahara was as fantastic as it was unexpected.

The final stage, a whopping 87 kilometres in one day, was waiting for us. Actually, this looming ultimate step had fuelled our conversations throughout the week. We were all very nervous, because the task seemed impossible, and the effort we would need was inconceivable. I had already lost a lot of weight, the fatigue had settled into my bones, I was starving, and my leg muscles did not want to respond anymore.

Our departure was set for precisely 7 a.m., like the four previous days. We sent the order to our brains, and our survival instinct did the rest. Supported by the concept of anticipatory regulation, we all instinctively started the day at a slower pace. Mentally programmed for a finish line 87 kilometres away,

I reached the 40 kilometre mark with the impression that I had barely begun the race, and I still felt fresh and ready to run.

The week had still done its job; the last 20 kilometres were extremely painful. The sun set early in the evening, which would have allowed us to run in much more comfortable conditions, were it not for our exhaustion. I had a burst of energy somewhere between kilometre 70 and kilometre 80 and launched myself forward into a sprint to insert myself into the head of the group. Seven kilometres from the finish, drained by the effort, I floundered. The sprint was probably not a good idea, and I lost all the ranks I had won.

As another stroke of bad luck, the batteries in my headlamp, also exhausted by the preceding days, died just one hour from the finish line. The night became very dark. Glow sticks were placed at every 50 metres along the path, but I still had to figure out how to light my own way.

The only light source I had was a small, mandatory safety lamp attached to the back of my bag. I put this flashing red light on one of the front straps of my bag and continued to run in the flashes of that red light. I was completely exhausted, I was losing my mind, and the new lighting was not helping at all. In this flickering light, I spotted a few scorpions on the ground. I jumped over them, adrenaline immediately whipping me into a frenzy of energy. The image continued to flash in my mind in red and black. My imagination was playing tricks on me, because I kept seeing scorpions every-where, dozens of them, thousands of them! I ran and ran, until I reached the finish line. I finished the Sahara Race in 21st place among 134 participants, and it took me 13 hours to run the final stage of the race. Running 87 kilometres in among the toughest conditions in the world was without a doubt the most difficult day of my entire athletic career. It was much harder than a triathlon, and harder than any day I spent on Everest.

In fact, while I would go back to Everest, I'm not so sure I would run through the Sahara again. I walked through pain and misery over the last two kilometres, stumbling repeatedly on the rugged terrain. I spotted the faraway glimmer of the camp, but I had no energy to sprint, even knowing that the finish line was close. Still, as I crossed the finish line, I found the energy to raise my arms and celebrate my accomplishment. The greater the effort and sacrifices you make, the greater the rewards will be. There is always a price to pay to feel the joy of accomplishment. I was jubilant.

Looking around me, I noticed that the night was very dark. There was only one person at the finish line, one of the race organizers. There were no trumpets or drums, no frenzied crowd, no music, no festivities. Sitting on a plastic bucket, he had fallen asleep against the pole holding up the finish line marker. With a light hanging around his neck and a notebook to record finish times on his lap, he represented the full welcoming committee. He took my name and my number, and the time I had arrived, then he said, "Great, that's everything. Good night!" And that was it. There was no one to tell me how well I had done, how I was strong, inspiring, and persevering! Absolutely nothing!

This finish line was extraordinary. Once again, the experience forced me to look at the core of my intent. Why had I wanted to participate in this race? For glory, or for the opportunity to grow? If we set goals, we shouldn't imagine anyone is waiting at the finish line. If the goals still make us happy, then we will know that we are setting them for the right reasons. It's a sign that our motivation is internal, that our why is strong, that our process is focused on our own growth, and that our goals are truly our own. From that moment on, points of resistance are smaller than our why. We want to persevere, and our struggles bring pleasure and teachings.

The next day, day six, was a rest day. I would have loved to sleep in, but the heat, the pain of sore muscles, and especially hunger, prevented everyone from sleeping. The day after that, day seven, we returned to the Egyptian capital to finish the race with a symbolic five-kilometre run around the pyramids. Traditional music awaited us, as well as a small ceremony and, of course, some food, which we devoured.

Victoria, British Columbia

I said at the start that I don't have a magic formula for success. I stand by this statement. Of course, some of the same ingredients are found in many stories of success. The first step is certainly one of those ingredients. Failure, but especially the perception we have of it, is another. Perseverance is another, but how can we extract its essence? How can we find it, or produce it? I suggest cultivating perseverance with a why, with a reason that is bigger than the accomplishment, with something that will serve everyone's progress rather than your own personal glory. I recommend small actions, because I believe in their power when they are consistent. A small action every day, a habit for growth aligned with your goal, that's what will take you wherever you want to go.

Of course, there are also patience, effort, and work, fundamental values that unfortunately seem to be disappearing from our society, which expects instant gratification. I sometimes worry about the younger generation, who no longer knows how to wait, how to make compromises, or how to fail and get up again in order to reach their goals. You would have every reason to call me a quack if I told you that anything is possible. Instead, my message is this: with years of effort, countless failures, and thousands of hours of work, one step at a time, almost anything is possible. Failure must be redefined as a point of resistance, as an opportunity for growth, and as a key ingredient that we welcome for growth.

My run across Canada ended on Friday, November 14, 2014, at 10 a.m., on Second Beach, over nine months after my departure. Hundreds of people were there on the beach to celebrate my arrival. I told dozens of media personalities and the whole country about what I wanted my journey to mean.

Just like the right to be on the starting line, benefits from the finish line must be earned. Forged with each step, the meaning of my campaign quietly came into being through the year. Most people discovered my campaign only when it was over, thanks to the media attention. It's ironic, but that's how things go. I could have wished that those thousands of people had discovered my project at the start, that they had followed my progress across the whole year on social media, that they sent me encouragements every day, that our posts had been liked and shared thousands of times, but that would just be my vanity talking. At the end of the day, the message of support for people with diabetes reached millions of people, and even if it was on the last day, that's all that matters.

November 14th was a very emotional day, as were the days that followed. Parties with the sponsors, interviews, and events of all kinds peppered our preparations to return to Quebec.

The trailer had to be cleaned and sold, which gave Patrick and me heartache. We had collected a lot of personal effects and souvenirs along the way. It was our home base, our oasis, our peaceful haven. Patrick would be returning to Quebec in the campaign truck, a last rite for him, and a final moment of solitude before returning to normal life. Meanwhile, I had to fly back to do more interviews in Quebec.

Slowly, families and friends returned home. Interview requests stopped, and my life slowed down. The trailer left with its new owner. Everything Patrick and I had decided to keep was packed into the back of the truck. It was the end of a dream, of a year spent in the great outdoors on the road with my best friend, always supported by people and the love that had followed us throughout our adventure. The introspection began gradually. Patrick and I had just spent a year together, hour after hour, but each in our own solitude, separated by a windshield during the day. We had no idea what the future would hold.

The following Tuesday, we were still in the city of Vancouver. Far from the spotlight, we took the ferry to Vancouver Island, home to Victoria, the provincial capital, and the 0 mile marker where the Trans-Canada Highway officially begins. Since Victoria is a small city, Vancouver was the obvious choice for our official arrival. From the ferry, I ran the 35 kilometres that separated me from the 0 mile marker, knowing that this time, they really would be the last. Patrick drove those 35 final kilometres by my side at 10 kilometres per hour. We arrived at the park and at the statue of Terry Fox that marks the start of the highway at about 3 p.m., alone, without fanfare. Nearby, a staircase leads to the shore and the Pacific Ocean. We headed down to the shoreline, which was quite calm on that sunny November afternoon. I stretched out on the stones while Patrick went for a walk, eventually settling down a dozen metres from me. We sat there in silence, contemplative, quietly accepting that we had reached the end.

Thirty minutes later, without discussing it, we automatically stood up at the same time, and we headed home.

Sébastien Sasseville gives talks at companies and organizations of all kinds and all sizes. Since 2015, he has given over 500 talks in Canada, North America, Europe, and Asia in both English and French, including a TEDx talk.

Sébastien Sasseville works closely with your team to create a unique and personalized talk, adapted to reflect your reality and to match your goals and challenges.

The core themes of his message are change management, leadership, teamwork, resilience, and purpose.

To contact the author:

www.sebinspires.com

info@sebinspires.com

seb@sebinspires.com